CONNECTION

THE CURRENCY TO HAPPINESS

Access Your Happiness. Right Here. Right Now!

LINDA TOMAI DUONG

Praise for Connection - The Currency to Happiness

Linda's wonderful anecdotes shared throughout this book tug gently on the heartstrings and serve to remind us to not only be kind to others but, also and above all, to be kind to ourselves. Her generosity of spirit and warm retelling of her family stories and personal experiences nudge us to pause from our busyness, take a deep breath, remember the good things in life, practice gratitude and gain a greater understanding and connection with our inner self. What a gift!

— Amanda W.

Read through your Introductory Chapter and it is amazing. It resonates so much with what I do as well especially when it comes to living one's purpose....I even made a video and "Setting Up For Lasting Happiness" and posted it on my channel on YouTube. Well done and looking forward to reading the full version!!!

— Olayinka O. PhD.

All I can say is Wow.... Your writing of your life journey to achieve your dreams was fantastic. Not only you amaze me of what you done and achieved but you touch my heart and inspire me too. I give my hats off to you! Just Amazing!

— Susan L.

Foreword

I have really enjoyed reading *Connection - The Currency to Happiness*. It has answered some of my questions and given me some insights already. You give good advice, Linda, and supported with personal experiences throughout and so it is very easy to read.

A lot of people will find something and probably lots of things that will help them. I did right to the end... Also, I enjoyed the way you interspersed the story with examples of your experiences, but also allow the reader to find a companion as they read through and you accompany and support the reader as they work through the book.

It poses questions that make me ask myself the same questions... and asked question begs to be answered. So I am hooked to find out answers as I read. I really enjoy your writing style and your story telling. Can't wait to read more of your books.

Happiness is something that I have longed for on years past... Your book is right and speaks truthfully. Happiness does come from within.

I like the five key areas - the five Fs, and think that although founded when you were a child, it is a pretty advanced formula as it accommodates all of life's main values. It is logical and sensible and gives the reader basic and essential groundwork upon which they can build happiness. It is definitely very real. So very readable. Reading your story is relaxing for me :)

The most important thing by far I think is the way these five keys provide a path that everyone can follow, especially as we can all relate it to the five fingers in our palm. For someone that is lost without any idea it provides a path with which they can proceed upon. For others, even successful people, it provides a template that they can fine tune their lives so that they can apply the model and expand each key area and that they can truly reach fulfilment. It did answer and fulfil some long standing questions that have plagued me for a long time... the idea of achieving happiness being the main one. Your whole book is like medicine to my soul...

I was facing a real dilemma years ago and if I had your book back then... earlier even, it could have saved me from a whole lot of grief...

Musician/Songwriter Rob W Stow

ISBN: 978-0-6481904-1-7

1st edition, October 2017

Printed in Sydney, Australia

Proceeds from the sale of this edition of the book; Connection – The Currency to Happiness will be supporting the following charities:

A Children's Foundation for the children cancer patients in Sydney.

A Foundation that builds school for the children in Uganda.

Orphanage in Vietnam – this is to continue what my mum did.

Cataract surgery in Vietnam – this is also to continue what my mum did.

Dedication

To my beloved mum,

Although you are no longer here, your love and strength continue to radiate and warm the hearts of those who continue to reach out to you. Your deep desire to wish for eternal happiness for all is what inspired this book.

You are an amazing mum and an incredible individual in your humble way. All the great things you do, you do so humbly and quietly. Your depth of love for the world lives on. Your depth of knowledge and wisdom to encourage others to strive for eternal happiness is what inspired me to carry on your mission and vision in igniting each individual's inner peace. I truly believe, that is ultimately, the path to world peace.

What I share in this book does not come near to reflecting your contribution to this family, to our extended relatives and the community. Your dedication to raising funds has helped build bridges, and made the lives easier for so many, especially for the orphanages and those who needed eye operations but had no means to, in Vietnam.

It was a challenge to articulate in English all the thoughts and values I have learned from you and dad, and from other cultures, especially Chinese, Vietnamese and Australian. I have worked hard to relay the values, wisdom, and teachings I learned over the years. I hope I have done justice to the challenge. With this book I am taking a leap of faith, doing it with imperfect actions to share your teachings, which have brought me happiness and true inner peace throughout these years, even when I was faced with life's challenges. It is my belief that what you have taught me is beneficial to others as well and that is why I am writing this book to share with all.

It is also my intention to pass on your legacy to your 24 grandchildren and nine great-grandchildren (at the time of writing this book, as more great-grandchildren are likely to come).

Table of Contents

Introduction

Are You There Yet?

Are you there yet? What are you seeking at the moment? What are you searching for? Is it financial success or the PHD? Is it a partner to share your dreams with? Or, is it to have the celebrity status that gives you millions of fans and followers on social media? If so, what does it mean to you once you have achieved that? Will that equate to happiness? If so, how long will this happiness last? And when will you feel truly happy so that you can *stop searching and be ultimately happy?* Be truly happy from the inside out...? The kind of happiness that enables you to feel true contentment, the kind that allows you to feel secure, loved, connected, calm, and alive with inner joy and inner peace?

Many people still believe that achieving financial success will mean happiness. Others believe it to be the goal in finding their dream partner. For still others, it is attaining that longed for beach house or the super fancy sports car. Do you believe that when you have achieved financial success and found your other half, or bought your dream house and the fancy sports car that you will have it all, and happiness will prevail?

Inevitably, there will come that moment when the goals that you have worked so hard to achieve will appear to be an illusion. Achievements and possessions can disappear or be taken away at a moment's notice, and with it, your happiness. Ultimately, you still won't feel complete and there will still seem to be something missing even after you have achieved all of those *external layers of happiness.*

Happiness that is dependent on external factors can quickly be replaced by feelings of loss, frustration, anger, resentment or even sadness.

This is why millions of people around the world, at different stages of life, are still seeking unsuccessfully for what they think of as happiness, and are still feeling deeply, profoundly, empty at times. This search often causes people to throw away their so-called success after years of striving and attaining accomplishments. In some cases, even for those people who have finally found their soulmate, it is still not enough to enable them to say, they have found true happiness and *feel content, and to say that they have experienced true happiness from the inside out.* I have searched for a long time, for answers to these questions as to, how can we achieve happiness and how can we sustain it throughout our lifetime?

At the beginning, the search for happiness may look like this; I need to have a successful career, then, I will be happy. But then, I also need to have someone special to share my life and achievements with, so I have to find my soulmate, my other half. Once I have found my other half, *then*, this will be all I need. I will, *then*, be happy! Oh but wait, I must have my dream house too. *"Then, I'll be happy!"*

How many times have you heard someone say: "I'll be happy when I buy that beach house" or "I'll be happy when I have found my soulmate" or "I'll be happy when I earn a million dollars"?

"I will be happy when..." is a statement that seems to come with a set of conditions. Is it possible to be happy before we achieve all of our goals or before we meet that set of conditions? And will that happiness stay with you forever once you have achieved all of the goals that you have set out to achieve?

This book is written to guide you to think about *happiness and true contentment* in the simplest way possible. My goal is to encourage you to find your way to the true heart of personal happiness with very simple new habits to access happiness and true contentment. I realised that while *my purpose is to bring joy to others*, in achieving that, my goal here is to guide you to stay true to what happiness is; so, together, let's stay on purpose — the purpose of a human life, which is seeing the connectedness of all beings. We can particularly see happiness through the following connections: Self-connection, Connection with others,

Connection with nature and all beings, and ultimately with the universe at large, including the Connection for business, Connection for contributions — all of these areas of connection result in **Connection for happiness.**

Through reading this book, you will discover a new way of accessing happiness, a simple way to achieve happiness by choosing to ignite that feeling of inner joy and inner peace, your true heartfelt contentment, which does not depend on others or external circumstances to provide it. You will also discover a way to access and re-ignite your happiness immediately from within yourself, here and now.

"Happiness is Not a Destination."

- Linda Tomai Duong

Chapter 1

The Quest for Happiness

"The feeling of achieving happiness is too far a stretch if we keep depending on material things, other people, or a certain event in life. As long as we wait for happiness to come externally, it never will. Happiness is an inside job."

- Linda Tomai Duong

Imagine a situation where you have struggled and worked hard throughout your life, where you have finally achieved your goals and dreams. Maybe you have even found your life partner, own your perfect home, have a beach house and drive your dream car. How would you feel? By this stage, life is good, isn't it? Imagine also that, suddenly, BANG! Someone ran a red light and crashed into your new car! Oh no! There goes the happiness in an instant. Now what? The car needs to be repaired, and all the while, your frustration builds, and your resentment at the presumably absent-minded person who ran the traffic light causing all this stress and hassle, escalates.

What happens to happiness now if your happiness was dependent on owning that car? Are you still happy or are you unhappy? *Of course not!* No one is happy during these moments. Some may even feel rage in such situation. But then what...? Okay, perhaps if you go on holidays, go travelling, that will make you happier. So it's time to travel *to find some happier feelings.* How about you travel the world?

Being in a position where you can travel the world is one of the best positions anybody could ask for in life. As you travel, your horizons expand. It's great fun for a while but somewhere along that journey, tiredness catches up, and this feeling of emptiness kicks in! If you have your partner with you, it is slightly better. However, there still comes a time, when you both sit down and think; we have money, we have each other, and we are travelling the world, having fun together. This should be it! But why is it that you feel this little hole of emptiness inside?

Something is missing! What is it, you ask?

So you've achieved financial success. Tick!

You've found your soul mate; your life partner is with you. Tick!

Then what's wrong? What's missing?

Most of us are aware that there is an essence that keeps our spirit bright, makes us feel alive, and motivates us to move forward in life. Yet, what is this missing essence? On the surface, it seems *happiness*; the feeling of being happy, is what we are searching for. But really, what is the *real* thing that has set millions of people in search for all their lives, throughout the millennia? As we know, many people have achieved their goal of becoming a millionaire but still their hearts are aching and yearning to fill this hole of emptiness inside.

Surely, it is possible that we are happy at certain moments in our daily lives, but *the state of being happy fluctuates throughout our lifetime.* Being happy is a feeling, an emotion that we feel, and emotions change from one moment to another, and from day to day.

In one moment, we can be happy, yet in another, we can feel frustrated and grumpy due to some external triggers such as an accident or a bad day at work. It is tricky to attain true happiness, and how do we achieve happiness so that it remains a constant element in our daily lives?

Since the feeling of *being happy* is in such a fluid mode, it is sometimes difficult to attain, and most people find the ability to experience *happiness* as a stable and lasting feeling elusive at best.

Feelings and emotions can be thought of like water in the ocean, it can be calm until the current comes along and gives it a ride and explodes into spectacular waves when it hits the rocks on the beach, or at the shore. When we are super excited or super angry, that is when an explosion of emotions happens, just like the ocean waves. There are days I felt like I was "dancing" on top of the waves and others, I feel like I have been pummelled and almost drowned by those very same waves.

However, as my day pans out, I still want to be able to *access* happiness and *retain it*, so that it gives me a stable and grounded feeling most of the time. I'm searching for that secure feeling that stays with me regardless of what happens in my life. It is a deeper emotion that remains in the core of my heart, a feeling that does not fluctuate due to my external circumstances. *This feeling is inner peace.* This is the feeling that allows me to feel settled, regardless of what is happening to the world around me.

As life goes on, things happen, and sometimes un-pleasurable events cause unhappiness, so I have been inspired to find ways to replace those disruptive moments with pleasurable moments as quickly as I can, or to look for ways to create a new foundation that will allow joy to happen again. This enables me to fall back into balance as soon as possible, to bring myself back to a harmonious state where I can reconnect to life's contentment before I drift too far off, so that I can feel happy again.

Over the years, the practice of this process has helped me to navigate life events and turn those unfavourable moments into learning journeys, just like road blocks appearing on the road, that force us to quickly find an alternative route so that we can move on, to continue our journey.

It is time we stop looking outside at superficial and material things, and start turning inwards and looking at our connections with ourselves, our relationships, with nature and the universe as we continue our search for happiness.

TIPS:

As you search for your happiness, whenever you feel overwhelmed or the need for a break, stop. Take a deep breath and exhale slowly. Close your eyes to feel centred and become grounded; then take three long, slow, deep breaths before you continue again. This simple exercise has profound effects and will help you to feel recharged and refreshed momentarily before the tension escalates.

"The feeling of achieving happiness is too far a stretch if we keep depending on material things, other people, or a certain event in life. As long as we wait for happiness to come externally, it never will. Happiness is an inside job."

Linda Tomai Duong

Chapter 2

The Discovery Journey

"Today, I don't need to be at a church, a synagogue or a temple in order to access inner peace, and nothing can take that feeling of inner peace and inner joy away from me."

- Linda Tomai Duong

People from all walks of life, from different religious faiths, from academic as well as non-academic fields, have travelled across the globe in search of happiness, spending extensive amounts of time searching, researching and exploring ways to attain this feeling called *happiness.*

Some amazing people have devoted themselves to do mountaineering, climbing the highest mountains on earth, in a quest to replace the emptiness with *that ultimate missing essence, called happiness,* claiming: "I will *ultimately* be happy for the rest of my life when I am on top of that mountain!" Some have worked so hard that they have reached the peak of the mountain, but, in the end, cannot get back to safety to enjoy what they have conquered. Others, as soon as they get back to land, they are climbing back on those same mountains again, irrespective of all that hard work and enduring unbearable weather conditions, exerting themselves, and risking their lives yet again.

They are continuously seeking to feel that special feeling that was somehow left behind on the peak of those mountains. What is this *ultimate* feeling that they are trying to attain? I can only assume it is a very deep emotion that not even their loved ones can provide. For them to make the decision to leave their loved ones behind, to experience such dangerous conditions, my guess is that it must be the *ultimate connection* that they feel up there, at the peak of the mountains, regardless of how horrendous the weather is. They seek that connection that no other human being or even a soulmate can provide, the feeling that they hope to hold on to for the rest of their lives, the kind of emotion that stays deep inside them and lasts for as long as their memory can hold. This mountaineering quest has been their perspective of the *ultimate happiness*. While in reality, it is the *connection to the universe* up there that they were truly seeking. The mountains elevate the spirit and soul of those who stand below, offering a very unique kind of connection. The universe is quite magical. And I have experienced many little magical moments myself, which I will share later in this book and in future books.

This quest for happiness by so many also reminds me of Buddha, who spent his whole life searching for enlightenment.

According to the *Oxford Dictionary*, the word 'enlightenment' means the action or state of attaining or having attained spiritual knowledge or insight, in particular, (in Buddhism) the awareness that frees a person from the cycle of rebirth.

Although I was born into a Buddhist family, I currently do not practice that religion nor any other for that matter. However, the philosophical teachings of Buddhism draw me to it, and I have simplified my understanding of *enlightenment* to mean; *to be awakened.*

When my church-going friends talk to me about their religion's teachings and beliefs, I can understand and respect their religion's teachings. We often share common values and, although I am not involved in the study of religion, it seems Buddhism and the overall story of Buddha, as well as my mum's great example, have offered profound and powerful inspiration for my own *quest for happiness.*

The inspirations of Buddha, my mum and many others in search for happiness were like a seed that had planted in my mind since early childhood that began to sprout in 1985 when I was about 15 years old, when I immigrated to Sydney, Australia.

At the time, my attention and thoughts became focused and intensified by my mum's inspiring actions. She was very dedicated to going to temple and doing charity work. She was also determined to follow Buddha's footsteps in seeking enlightenment so that she could join him in Nirvana when that day came for her to leave this physical world. *She was making a very conscious choice — to be happy even after she leaves this earth.*

Coupled with my unlimited curiosity, yet, limited teenaged knowledge of the story of Buddha and his search for enlightenment, I asked the following questions:

Why did Buddha want to seek a way to free a person from the cycle of rebirth?

Is it perhaps that Buddha viewed life as a suffering path and therefore, his view was that, there were no benefits in rebirthing into a new life, only to have to go through the same sufferings again?

Did that mean that Buddha was seeking *ultimate happiness*? Was Buddha seeking the kind of happiness that lasts even when unfavourable life events happen? Seeking those feelings and emotions that remain no matter what happens? The feeling that remains deep in the core of your heart and soul, which I have discovered to be *inner peace...*

Growing up as a Chinese-Vietnamese child, I was surrounded by stories of the sufferings brought upon the people by the wars in Vietnam and the stories of the Japanese war. I constantly heard how people wished that life could be different, better and *happier*. People around me *yearned* for happiness.

Everyone was constantly searching for a better life. I felt their eagerness and sadness, motivation and despair all at the same time; the eagerness and enthusiasm to seek happiness as well as their pain and struggle in everyday life. Fortunately, I was sheltered and protected, especially compared to the people around me who were less fortunate. I was blessed with safety and even some luxuries such as having Pho — the Vietnamese beef noodles. A dish that we think of as an economical one nowadays. However, it wasn't so back then, and it seems, this dish is best cooked in Australia because we have the best beef here. Yummolicious!

Perhaps, being sheltered and unharmed was the state of mind that had freed me from pain and suffering, and allowed me to observe, wonder, and ponder about life ahead of me, ahead of us.

I grew up in the 1970s with black and white TV, hearing stories of the unjust system that pained the Vietnamese people's hearts and souls. I had friends that have gone through the war time, whom had actually survived walking through a mine field. I also witnessed many people, including people I knew, who were jailed unjustly for trying to find ways to make life a little better.

When you grow up in such a chaotic environment with such experiences at such a young age, it is inevitable that with these memories in the back of your mind, that one day you too will go searching for *happiness*. Much like Buddha and my mum, I too, was searching for my 'Nirvana', my eternal happiness. It was as if the task was handed to me at a very young age. The baton was bestowed upon me and the quest for happiness had begun as early as I could understand the stories told to me, as early as I could comprehend the sufferings of others. Tears are rolling down my face as I type these words with memories of those emotions; the pain and frustrations of others around me. I felt them then, I feel them even now.

I understood spirituality as early as when I was five years old. Some people told me I had an *old soul*. Every night, I knelt next to my mum to pray for world peace. She prayed in Vietnamese, translated her words meant:

"I pray for peace for the world.

I pray that those who study will graduate.

I pray for us all to have a bright mind."

She did that every single night at 7:00pm, without fail. As a child I did not understand the meaning of those words but as I grew older, I realised that when she prayed for those who study to graduate, she was referring to both the academic field as well as the religious field.

At first, I understood its meaning only in term of relating to academic achievement and financial achievement. For students to graduate with good grades and great results at university so that they can get better jobs and be able to provide for their families financially.

As I grew up, I later realised that she was also praying and wishing for the religious students and other followers like herself, that once they 'graduated' in their religion, at the end of this physical life, they would be assured of joining Buddha in Nirvana, or whatever other afterlife they believed in. She wished for everyone to be at peace, even after this physical life. She wished for all to have *eternal* peace.

The more I think of this prayer, the more I feel moved by her eternal care for the world.

This prayer rings in my ears each time I think of her, and each time I remember how she prayed — her ocean's depth of love for the world. It was these examples that led me to think *out loud* at 15 years of age, and to find practical ways to keep myself happy, to seek out happiness in my daily life.

Little did I know that thousands of others before me had also sought for years on end to find happiness.

Inevitably, at different points in my late teens and early twenties, I would get frustrated and became impatient, but whenever I experienced low moods or felt unhappy emotions, I would go to the park or beach to seek my happiness in solitude, among nature.

At the time, I was living in the western part of Sydney, the largest city in Australia. Sometimes it would take me two hours each way, using public transport, to get to the north side of the city, to Manly Beach, my favourite place to be alone. Two hours each way was well worth it when I could come home with a peaceful heart, because the open air of the beach had brushed away all the tension of my heartache. It was an incredibly magical place for me. I felt as if I was able to converse with the universe and yet I didn't need to speak a word. That is the power of nature and the universe. I would come home feeling settled, somewhat content, relaxed and okay again.

Sydney has beautiful beaches and bushlands. After my walks along the beach or in the bush, I would then go to the libraries, as there was no internet yet, to search for books that might have answers for me. I did not know it back then, but these were called *self-help* books. I had no interest in, and no time for novels. I only read those books that could help provide answers to my situational problems.

Each time, I selected a stack of books, sometimes as many as 20, flipping through them, picking out the chapters that somewhat applied to my situation, reading parts of many chapters, until it was time to return them. Even if I only read two or three of the books I borrowed, it was as if the words from all the other books crept into my mind on their own. By the time I had to return the books, it felt as if all my questions and problems were answered and resolved.

I discovered that this was because we each have a *higher-self*. If we can just be patient and consult our inner guide instead of seeking external places, we will eventually find the answers we seek within ourselves. Only we know ourselves best so when we *tune in* and connect with ourselves, we will almost always find the answers within ourselves.

Over the years, I have done a lot of soul searching. I would choose a peaceful location to sit and avoid the noisy world outside, so that I could think and quieten my conscious mind so that I can "hear" the universe as I asked the questions that no one else could help me answer. I turned to the universe when no one could understand what I was thinking. I observed the thoughts that come into my mind and I continued to tune in and listen to my subconscious mind, and that was when I discovered *my higher-self*. I learned this daily practice at an early age from my mum and other elders in the neighbourhood. I have spent a lot of time people watching and I sometimes look at people very intently, without realising that I am doing it. I don't mean to be rude, but it seems as if I fall into a *daydreaming* state. It appears to others that I may be staring at people, when in actual fact my mind has drifted off somewhere else, daydreaming away, searching for answers. Have you done that before?

"Happiness is all about feelings and understanding our own emotions and so the best way to achieve happiness is to feel happy inside and by connecting to that feeling."

— *Linda Tomai Duong*

Many people search for happiness through financial success or academic theories. Given my situation when I was still young, I did it by observing and connecting to other people's emotions. I have always been curious about people's feelings and emotions, and that is why I love engaging with people of all ages. I love it as much as I love my alone time at the beach, at the park, bush walking or mountain climbing. Simply connecting with people, nature and the universe - the *connection* is what I love. I thrive when I connect with others. Every time I feel tired, exhausted or I am running low on energy, I either take a walk to *connect with nature* or I call a friend and talk and make that human *connection*. Connecting with nature and other people helps me to feel recharged, rejuvenated and refreshed.

No doubt, like so many other people, you have also tried to find the answer to *happiness* at some point or other. Have you wondered, pondered and questioned what will give you the happiness you seek? Like me and many others, have you ever felt like leaving everything behind because what you had been working so hard for over the years, suddenly no longer worked, or no longer have any meaning? I have witnessed this many times in my life.

How long does a person need to experience the feeling of being happy in order to say *"Yes, I am truly happy?"* How long does it take for someone to feel that they have achieved happiness?

One person's answer is different than another's. Some people need to have a big beach house and be famous before they can say that they are completely happy. But what happens when that house gets damaged by a natural disaster?

For me, happiness can be the simple joy of appreciating nature, the sun, a beautiful flower, the free air — feeling that freedom in the air, the calmness, and the sound of birds singing. *I have come to appreciate that the sun gives life.* If you come from a place where there is not much greenery, you can understand my appreciation for such simple things.

However, suddenly, all of those joyful feelings can change, and be swept away by sad news such as the passing of a friend, or the shock and sadness I felt when my mum passed away while she was away on holidays in Vietnam. Such emotional events can affect us for days, months and even years. When your happiness is taken away like that, does that mean that you will never feel joy or be happy again even when you see the flowers or hear the birds sing?

Amazingly, for me, that sense of simple joy, of appreciating nature did come back, and I am again able to experience those little *happiness* moments in life, to still see the beauty in life, because nature has the power to heal and cultivate appreciation and gratitude. But at the same time, it doesn't mean that I will never feel the loss of my dear mum again. It has been more than a decade now since her passing, and *I still miss her dearly*, more so as each day goes by, because as I grow older, I understand more and more, of the valuable lessons she had taught me. I appreciate their meaning on a much deeper level than when I was younger.

These days, as I reflect on all that she had taught me, I feel as if I am connecting to her at an even deeper level than ever before. As I try to pass on to my children the stories and lessons that she had taught my siblings and I. I become even more thankful of the meanings of those lessons and the wisdom she had shared. It brings a profound level of gratitude and gratefulness, and a sense of appreciation that brings joy to my heart and allows me to feel connected to her through the memory of her teachings.

As my search for *happiness* continues, I have come to realise that, the momentary feeling of being happy is not exactly the same as *true happiness*. The feeling of being happy in itself is not the indication by which we can determine whether or not we have achieved *happiness*.

The true happiness that I am seeking is a more stable feeling; one that does not fluctuate. Instead, it stays steady in the core of my heart and mind. I really wanted to experience a more solid and steady state of calmness; *the feeling of being at peace* —that feeling of *deep inner peace* that we have heard of from the great masters and monks. However, this concept of *inner peace* is often presented in such an exclusive manner that it feels as if, it is impossible to achieve on a daily basis unless you are a monk, nun, spiritual leader, or philosopher.

I'm seeking a status that allows me to feel truly contented and able to experience the peace from within myself, and to experience inner joy; that elated feeling inside me since my early childhood days, regardless of whether or not I have achieved my goals. I aim to achieve that grounded calmness, the inner peace and the natural state of pure joy that we were born with, an emotion that can be accessed at any given time, and a sense of being at peace on a daily basis, regardless of our external circumstances. As I share the following experience, it will help me to articulate the feeling I have been searching for.

The sudden passing of my mum was a very emotional and shocking experience. It could have been enough to spiral me into a state of misery for a long time, as I was very, very close to her. I could still cry on her shoulder even in my thirties. I still remember it as if it was yesterday, after a difficult and challenging day at work when I was new and struggling to establish my new bridal boutique and running the business.

One day after work, I picked my mum up from the shops on the way home, we were still in the car, parked in the driveway when I just turned to her and burst into tears on her shoulder. I didn't need to say a word and she didn't say anything either but she understood that my tears were from the stress and exhaustion of working long, hard hours. During the first few months of establishing my business, it was very demanding, not only because it was a new business that required a lot of hard work, with many challenges and obstacles, but also because it was moving into the busy season, as well as the load of preparing for my own wedding. I worked extremely hard every night until almost dawn, hence my physical and emotional exhaustion.

My mother, my mentor, my greatest teacher and best friend had passed away suddenly on a vacation trip in Vietnam a few years after I got married. She was waiting to meet my babies but I wasn't ready. My children never got to meet her. I did not get to see her again after sending her off at Sydney's airport. That was the last time I was with her. She went to sleep and never woke up again. She had suffered from a heart condition and had a pacemaker but the doctor had said she was doing great and that she was well enough to travel again. She loved travelling and devoted herself to doing charity work between Sydney, Australia, and Ho Chi Minh, Vietnam.

When I received the sad news of her passing, the first thing came out of my mouth was "But, the cardiologist said she was okay to travel! What happened?" I refused to accept my new reality. I said to the family doctor, "I am going to fly there to check it out; they must have made a mistake!" I was actually picturing her just lying there in her bed, that the doctors had made a huge error, and that I could tell them in person that they had made a serious mistake, which they need to re-examine her and somehow give her the right medication so that she would wake up again.

Upon arriving at Ho Chi Minh City airport, my husband and I were greeted by our family and taken straight to the temple. There, lay my mother, looking peaceful, dressed as she had instructed us six months prior, that in the event her last day on earth comes; those were the departing clothes we were to dress her in. I looked at her. I looked at my siblings. Everything was prepared and ready for the funeral ceremony. I was speechless. I did not know whether I was dreaming or whether it was actually happening. I felt too disoriented to know what reality was and what not.

I was suddenly transported to a different place, as if I had time-travelled to the future. While on the plane to Vietnam, I convinced myself that everything was going to be okay, I would see her again. I was wearing my mother's and my favourite cardigan; mine was pink and hers was grey. She had taken hers with her, when she had left for Vietnam. As I walked into the temple, I was scolded. "How could you be wearing pink to such an occasion?" I really felt like screaming: "I was not preparing to attend a funeral!" except no words came out. Traditionally, white is the appropriate colour to wear to a Buddhist funeral, and so I just took off the pink cardigan quietly with my head down.

Fortunately, I was wearing a white shirt and white pants underneath my pink cardigan, and those were more appropriate colour for the occasion.

Somehow, I had been imagining that I would pick my mum up from the hospital and that we would go home together. This is not the scene that I had imagined! I felt like kicking and screaming: "This is not right! I want my mum back! They must have made a mistake!" but no words came out. There was a huge lump in my throat. Yet, despite my grief and despair, as I looked down at my mum's peaceful face, amazingly, *I felt her peace.*

That peace overtook the shock and disorientation within me. The peacefulness that I felt from looking at her, communicated directly to my heart, telling me that although she may no longer be here physically, she would *always be in my heart* and *I could still communicate with her* whenever I want.

It was then that I realised that although I had lost her physical presence, I was not totally *disconnected* from her. I felt that I could still communicate with her, somehow, if I wanted to, and that gave me a profound sense of reassurance, calmness and solace. Even though I was there with the rest of my family, that *inner peace* was what provided me with comfort and peace.

I recalled the doctor had said she was okay to travel, but she had overworked herself while overseas. She had been doing her charity work and was a totally dedicated individual, and a very devoted Buddhist. She went to temple regularly in Sydney and helped raise funds in Australia for a charity in Vietnam to help the blind — those who have cataracts but could not afford eye operations, and to help the orphanages. One night after all the work was done, she went to sleep and never woke up again. I never got to see her in person again. I could have been very upset and angry, very bitter, or worse!

My mother, my mentor, my forever best friend is gone and I can never cry on her shoulder or hug her again. I still cry every time I think of her, and my children often come and give me hugs when this happens. Even now, as I type these words a big lump has formed in my throat. I really, really, miss her physical presence. Tears are rolling down, it is 3:00am as I sit and type these words. Hubby and the kids are asleep and all is quiet. I miss my mum dearly and so wish that she was here, alive so that I could tell her: "Mum! I was runner up in the Toastmaster's International speech contest at my club level!" but she's not here. She would have been proud to hear her quiet and shy daughter earning such an award. From where we were back then, you're not supposed to speak your mind. There was no such things as 'show and tell' or public speaking in the school years. After coming to Sydney, I spoke no words of English, we would have never imagined that I do public speaking.

Instead of feeling misled by the doctor or losing faith and feeling bitter, I feel peace. I feel connected with her through the happier memories and the legacy she has left behind. However, all of these feelings are only possible *because* I allow myself to be in the present moment, in order to be connected to these feelings and emotions that are surfacing.

"We need to be OK to be alone, to allow the time and space in our minds and hearts, to feel our emotions, in order to connect to the feelings we are experiencing. This will help us to be opened to receive deeper emotions as we connect to ourselves and others both physically and emotionally and even soulfully."

— *Linda Tomai Duong*

Throughout the many years of my mum's guidance and teaching, I have found true *inner peace* and *inner joy* in remembering our good times instead of being angry at the loss of her. I am still teary each time I think of her and I still cannot hold back the tears, the deep emotions of missing her, but I still feel connected to her very much. She exemplifies something so powerful that I aim to teach my children as they grow, and I hope to share these insights with you through the pages in this book.

"It is the power within us that gives us strength – the invisible strength of self-connection is what brings us peace; the ultimate happiness."

— *Linda Tomai Duong*

The ability to connect with ourselves, with our own inner self-presence, with others, with nature and all beings, and with the universe and even with our loved ones that are no longer here with us, is what helps connect us to our own inner peace and inner joy.

Once you have acquired this practice of deep connection, you will feel amazing strength; you will find more meanings in the things you see and experience, you will be able to face life events better, and most of all, you will never feel alone again. You can then access this deep emotional strength to look after others and be contributing to others better. It really opens up your heart and you will feel larger than life itself.

It is my wish that you will achieve this *inner strength* after reading this book.

Remember, you need to be okay to be alone, to allow some time to open your heart and mind, in order to experience and be connected to the feelings you are experiencing. This will help you to stay open to receive more deeply as you connect to others physically, emotionally and soulfully.

"Quietness is one of the most precious element in nurturing the mind to activate its power."

— Linda Tomai Duong

TIPS:

Every Morning: Stand up and stretch your arms out sideways with your palms facing upwards and take three slow, conscious breaths. Exhale slowly. Think of three positive things that you look forward to. It can be anything as small as meeting a friend at the bus stop or as big as signing a deal at work. Anything you can look forward to.

Every Night: Do the same as in the morning. Stand up and stretch your arms out sideways with your palms facing upwards and take three slow, conscious breaths. Exhale slowly. Think of three things that went well or that you appreciate and are grateful for this day. Again, it can be anything as small as having a nice chat with a friend at lunch time or as big as getting a pay raise. Anything you feel gratitude for.

As time goes on and your new habit builds, you can extend the time to as long as you like. This is a simple way to center your mind, to set the positive intentions and focus to begin your day, and to calm your thoughts and emotions at the end of the day. This is also described as Centering or Mindfulness.

Usually, centering is done before yoga or meditation is practiced. By doing this quick centering exercise, you are bringing yourself to the present moment, to a mindfulness state, and to a short moment of relaxation, while at the same time letting the universe know that you are ready to receive its guidance by having your palms stay open. This practice will help you to receive more love, more joy and more happiness, be it through friendships, family, or financial success and other personal goals.

At this point, let's take a pause and take three deep slow breaths to feel connected with ourselves before we move on.

"You don't need to be at a church, a synagogue or a temple in order to access inner peace, and nothing can take that feeling of inner peace and inner joy away from you."

Linda Tomai Duong

Chapter 3

Achieving True Contentment and Happiness

"True contentment comes from the place of truly feeling inner peace and inner joy."

— Linda Tomai Duong

Acquiring the emotional, mindful, and soulful connection is how we access our own inner peace and inner joy. *Inner peace and inner joy is where true contentment and happiness resides.* This was the feeling I had been searching for throughout my growing years, consciously and unconsciously. It is the feeling that enables me to feel true happiness and contentment now regardless of what happens externally.

This kind of happiness is not the happy feeling on the surface like eating ice cream or driving a sports car. It is the deeper sense of the simple yet profoundly joyful moments that come from meaningful connections, be it with yourself, others, nature and all beings. Such as the moment you hear a bird sing, when you see the raise of the break of dawn, or the moments that were walking down the road and you saw someone who needed a hand controlling her shopping trolley on a slippery sidewalk and you saved her from slamming into someone else's car. Remember how it left you feeling a little proud of yourself for helping a stranger? Those are little moments of happiness that are just simple and joyful, that give us contentment within ourselves.

So, what is contentment?

According to the *Oxford Dictionary,* contentment is a *state of happiness and satisfaction.*

According to my search for happiness, we need to feel the contentment in order to say we are truly happy. Happiness has been studied for years on end, and to this date we are still searching. Isn't it time to look at happiness with a different perspective? Can we come to realise that the ultimate happiness is actually a true contentment that we feel deep inside, not something that comes from external sources, nor is it from material achievements, financial status or from another person? This true contentment comes from the place of really feeling *inner peace and inner joy.*

Inner peace and inner joy is an internal feeling that needs to be nurtured and cultivated by activating and accessing our own inner feelings and deep emotions by connecting to ourselves, embracing the feeling and appreciating it. We cannot achieve happiness by expecting it from outside sources, nor from another person. Neither from our partners, our siblings, and/or our children. Children can bring us amazing joy when they are young. However, when they have grown up and have their own lives they can still bring us joy but we cannot *expect* it from them.

We need to start with ourselves, by connecting to our inner-self. This includes tuning in and listening to our intuitive thoughts and feelings. It's about practicing reflective thinking to connect with our thoughts and feelings, to gain deeper contentment.

Reflective thinking is a skill I learned very early in Vietnam. When my mum used to share her thoughts shown us how she does her reflective thinking, such as: "We do it this way, and we don't do it that way" or "Things work out better this way compared to that way" et cetera.

When I first came to Sydney, Australia, I didn't have enough vocabulary in English to articulate what I wanted to say and so I used to say that I often do self-assessment, when in actual fact what I was trying to say was reflective thinking.

Later on, when I studied primary teaching (a degree I am yet to complete), I also learned the term meta-cognition, which was discussed among the educational psychology subjects, and it means; awareness and understanding of one's own thought processes, it also means to think about your thinking.

This simply means tuning into your own thoughts to gain clarity with your own thought process. Once we have done that, we will be able to connect with each other better, and feel the joy in connecting with each other more meaningfully. When we are able to connect with other better, we will be more content and relaxed. Being relaxed will naturally lead us to connect with nature and other beings, and the universe at large.

We can begin with such simple activities as a walk in nature, a run in the park, or a swim in a pool or at the beach to relax and let go of the *busyness* in life. For example, we begin with a walk to clear our minds so that we can connect with ourselves. That helps us connect well with others, nature and all beings, and the universe. As we connect, we will realise that it is a big circle of connection. In the end, it comes back reflecting back to us with a loving world. That is when circle of connection is completed, allowing us to feel oneness with the universe.

Being able to appreciate simple beauties; such as a flower or an encounter with an animal, watching and listening to the waves at the beach; such experiences offer us opportunities to see the beauties in life and experience a deeper sense of calmness and gratitude in our hearts.

It is important to respect and acknowledge the value of all beings. You, yourself are deserving the most of all respects and have unmeasurable value and much the same is considered for all the living things around us.

What I am emphasising is that we need to respect the worthiness in ourselves and in all beings with special attention to ourselves. It is about maintaining and having self-respect and self-worth even when circumstances change, such as when there is no money left or when the beach house is gone. You can still have a sense of self-respect, inner calm and inner peace, perhaps even joy. Yes, you may even feel joy even when the beach house is gone, because the joy comes from appreciating that what you still have left is your*self*. You can be grateful that you are still alive and well even after disaster strikes because you know that when you are safe from harm, *you can rebuild anything*. Having inner strength is when *you* can empower yourself to feel that essence of true contentment, from the inside out. Nobody or anything can take that feeling away from you. With it, you can rebuild anything you want.

"Having inner peace and inner joy, you can rebuild everything and anything that you want."

— *Linda Tomai Duong*

Achieving Contentment through Solitary Time

"Solitude allows opportunities for creativity and beliefs to be realised. It helps us to build strength and power from within that allows us to focus, ponder, and to cultivate our mind's full potential."

— Linda Tomai Duong

I grew up with a lot of alone time, and solitary times for me were opportunities to think without outside distractions. I was a very inquisitive child and so I had many questions in my head. Solitary times were my golden moments. Throughout history, there have been many examples of great thinkers, philosophers, wise men and personal mentors who established how effective and powerful solitary time can be if well used.

My father moved from China to Vietnam and I was born in Ho Chi Minh City where we lived in a Chinese community in the nearby suburb of Chợ Lớn. Back in the 1970s, marbles and sticks were the most common toys for boys. Girls played a game similar to a version of Knucklebones, which consisted of five very small sand bags. Other favorite activities were catching baby fish in the ponds with fish nets. There were not a lot of things to keep children busy like nowadays.

The seniors would work until they could not work anymore and then they would sit around watching each other and the neighbourhood. They would observe the children playing, and other adults working. I learned at a very early age to enjoy my own solitary moments and it was those moments that allowed my mind to be curious and encouraged my creativity. Often, I would be the elders' audience, listening to their stories. From the collective wisdom of these elders, I learned valuable lessons that I would never have learned at school, allowing me to gain incredible lessons from their experiences. I witnessed their emotions as they shared their stories and teachings, such as this Cantonese proverb:

"食得咸鱼抵得渴"

Upon translation, this proverb means:

"Know the consequences and be prepared to pay the price, or take responsibility for your choices."

If I was to translate this phrase literally, it means: "If you dare to eat the preserved, salty fish, you must be able to put up with the thirst!" You see, in the ancient times, there were no refrigerators, so the fishermen would save up the fish they caught on the good days, preserving them in tubs of sea salt, so that during bad weather days, when they could not go out to sea to fish, they would have some saved up supplies. Of course, by then the fish would have become extremely salty and when you ate it you would become extremely thirsty, hence this Cantonese-Chinese wisdom, teaching us to be resilient and build strength as we go.

This wisdom has four levels of teaching. First, there is planning ahead. Think ahead of what to do for the rainy days. Second, be aware and be conscious of the actions you are about to take, such as, if you want to eat these salty fish, you need to be aware of the consequences. Third, we have to recognise the fact that we all have choices. You can choose to eat it or you can choose not to. However, once chosen, you must be prepared to face the challenges and the consequences accompanied by those choices. Finally, last but not least, in fact, *is the most important lesson of the teaching: endurance.*

Another Cantonese Proverb with great teaching is:

"三思而後行!"

Upon translation, this proverb means:

"Think thrice before you act."

To translate it literally, it means *"Think three times before you take the action!"* This wisdom teaches us to think carefully before acting, it brings about mindfulness and to be aware of the consequences that come with the actions we are about to take. With practice, this becomes a very effective habit in daily life as it requires you to be totally present.

Mindfulness is not something we can teach children easily but with this proverb, I can. I have translated this to teach my young children by saying: *"Thinking about what you are doing makes you smarter!*" This is my simple way to teach and encourage children to practice thinking about their actions and the consequences before they take the action, and it applies to adults too. A super simplified way of practising mindfulness.

I have come to realise that to be surrounded with the wise elders of my community at such a young age was truly a blessing. At the time, I thought I was doing them a favour by being their audience, lending them my ears, keeping them company and that, as such, it was for their benefit. As it turned out, *I* was the one who benefited and learned valuable life lessons. From then, I have also learned to listen with intuitive feelings. I discovered quietness is where I could find answers to my heart's burning questions.

Whenever you have a deep burning question that relates to personal issues or personal development, instead of letting it frustrate you or make you feel anxious to get immediate answers, just sit with it for a while and tune into your higher self. Often the answer comes, and when the answer comes from within, you will feel more content than the answer that was recommended by somebody else.

"The one who looks outside, dreams; the one who looks inside, awakes."

— Carl Gustav Jung

Solitude is what allowed me to dream at the age of five, that I wanted to make beautiful dresses when I grew up - to be a fashion designer, but back then in Vietnam, I had absolutely no clue of this term at all. All I knew was that I wanted to make beautiful dresses when I grew up. At the time, the ladies, mums and grandmas in the neighbourhood would frugally save scraps of fabrics, cutting out triangles and squares to make quilts. The idea was to save every inch of fabric available and turn it into something useful.

Others made casual clothing from new fabrics; tops and pants were the most practical, for everyone worked then, even children. The only people who didn't work were those that could not, such as the very young and the very old. The only ones in between that did not work had to be almost completely incapacitated and even *they* were amazingly creative with their limited abilities. For example, I once saw a man with no legs, who dragged himself across the ground on a piece of cardboard by laying on his side and using his arms so that he could get to a place where he could ask for spare change.

In those days, they had no wheel chairs. If all you have is your mind, you become very creative and resourceful. Everything was basic, simple, and all about functionality and survival. He moved about from place to place by laying sideway, extending one arm then dragging his body forward with the strength of his arm and elbow while using the other arm to push on the ground, almost like swimming freestyle except on the hard, dirty and sometimes muddy ground and not in the comfort of the water. He displayed incredible strength with the purpose of living on.

Anyway, back to sewing, most people made their own clothes or paid a seamstress to make the clothes for them. There were no shopping centres. A few male tailors made suits but not many made modern day dresses except the traditional Vietnamese dresses. So, I used to daydream quietly that I would make beautiful dresses when I grew up. I drew and created my own paper dolls that I could dress with tiny pieces of fabric scraps. The idea was extremely basic as I had never done much drawing. Yet, that dream lived on and after coming to Australia, I studied fashion design and eventually, in 2001, opened a bridal boutique where I offered personally designed wedding gowns and evening gowns.

I have also realised another dream during my solitary moments. When I was between seven and nine years old, my second eldest sister "*escaped*" Vietnam to look for a better life, just like many other Vietnamese refugees. Her story is one of surviving on a boat at sea and arriving as a refugee, and adjusting to a new life in Australia.

After she had arrived, we received stories of her survival at sea and adjusting to her new life. I would look forward to receiving her news from Australia and letters from my cousin in America. I used to sit and daydream, wondering: "What is America like?

What is Australia like? Is it the same as here in Vietnam?" There was no colour TV, no internet, and I had never seen a world globe or seen any world maps. I was also yet to study geography, so I had absolutely no idea at all about anything of the world outside, except the little area where I lived. So what did I do?

I sat and daydreamed.

Growing up, I was often told to "stop daydreaming!" Daydreaming was what led me to actually travel around the world after coming to Australia, even though I suffered very severe motion sickness. I couldn't go anywhere in Vietnam because anytime I travelled on a bus or boat, I would get very sick and so I was "*grounded*" at home while my other siblings were able to travel to other cities with my mum. I couldn't go anywhere and often stayed home with my dad. After coming to Sydney, I used to walk for one whole hour to get to school each way, there and back; whether it was pouring, raining days or freezing cold, windy days, because every time I travelled by car or bus, I vomited.

After immigrating to Australia, my motion sickness continued but my deep curiosity drove me out of my comfort zone to explore the world.

Interestingly, my motion sickness seemed to disappear as soon as I decided that I wanted to travel and see the world. I was so determined that even the first time I got on the plane, I travelled well! No vomiting, no headaches, not even dizziness. Such was the power of a determined mind.

But without my solitary times, I couldn't have done any of that. Solitude was what allowed my mind to wonder, to ask myself questions that I couldn't answer and those became the quest, the desire, and the dream waiting to be fulfilled.

Achieving Contentment through Being Alone

"You can go anywhere on your own, alone, and you don't feel lonely. The secret is to have connection with yourself."

— *Linda Tomai Duong*

Being alone is self-empowering. You will feel independent, strong minded, and have the sense of being unshakeable as you realise, "*I can do anything on my own!*"

During my trips, I was often asked, "*Are you here alone?*" Whether it was my first trip to Fiji when I was 21, or the trips I did up to when I was 46 years old, people always seemed so surprised that I was travelling *alone and happy!* They didn't seem to believe I could travel alone, even at the age of 28, probably due to my then "baby-face". On the flight to Alaska, an older man looked around to see if he could see my parents. In the end, he couldn't resist but had actually asked me; "Are you travelling to Alaska, alone?" That was back in 1998. On a more recent trip to

Hawaii in 2016, someone said to me towards the end of the day; *"I never knew you were on your own. I could never do that. And you're so happy!"*

I have never really needed a friend to accompany me when I went out. Don't get me wrong, I am not a loner. I love solitary time - but I also love connecting with others. I thrive on connecting and connections. Yet when I am alone, I get to appreciate the opportunity to connect with my own thoughts and feelings, and I also get to connect with my surroundings and other beings. For example, I often am in awe of how amazing the civil engineers are in cutting hills and mountains to make way for a canals, roads or railway lines, or the amazing tunnels under the sea, and the incredible bridges connecting us to places.

I get to nurture my inquisitive mind. That is what got me here, sharing with you how good it is to have time alone. If you ever have the opportunity to be alone, try not to keep yourself too busy so that you have time and space in your mind to connect with yourself and your surroundings. If you are not used to being alone, try to embrace it. You can start by having short quiet times to yourself then slowly stretching it out to be longer.

I have come to understand one of the reasons why we don't want to be alone is we think of the 'what ifs'. This tends to lend itself to a downward spiralling thought pattern very quickly, with thoughts of all kinds of things that could, or would, go wrong - making us feel uncertain and insecure. That's when we need 'hand-holding', back-ups, and some extra company to help us feel safe.

Instead of 'what ifs', I focus on my curiosity and my wonderment of what I want to do or see, immersing myself in whatever I am doing. For example, if I'm travelling to another country, instead of worrying about "what if I can't speak the language and that I may get lost", I would be thinking, "How shall I communicate with them when I don't speak their language?" This usually helps me brainstorm all sorts of ways to communicate such as using body language, pen and paper, et cetera. Being curious in imagining how the interactions will go is far more entertaining and elating than thinking of the negatives of 'what ifs'.

I don't remember ever felt lonely travelling on my own, because I was always connecting with people. At the same time, at the end of the day when I returned to my hotel room, I also enjoyed the quiet time to myself. I would write in my journals and postcards as back then it was still a popular thing to do, and reflect on what I saw during the day. I took time to savour the memories, looked at photos that I had developed on the trip. Back then it was still rolls of films that we used to develop photos. I also took the opportunity to appreciate the different languages spoken and the people I met, and appreciate the different cultures and the many sights that I enjoyed; simply appreciating seeing the world. If I was busy going to the bars and parties at night, I wouldn't have been able to do all of these self-nurturing, heart-warming, and mind growing activities that helped me to discover what happiness is to me. Enjoying solitary time is completely different than being anti-social, there is a significant distinction.

Enjoying your own company is a habit that you can develop at any age. It's never too late. Being able to enjoy your own company is very special as it allows you to go to many places without needing a company and creates moments where we get to be stretched, to get out of our comfort zones to meet new people, and even better, it allows you to experience the feeling of connecting with nature, your surroundings and all beings, that you would not have otherwise, if you had others accompanying you. I really do enjoy my surroundings wherever I travel to. My favourite trips have been to Alaska and Switzerland, travelling on a Rhine cruise and on a QEII (Queen Elizabeth II) cruise from Auckland, New Zealand, back to Sydney. These trips have gave me incredible experiences.

When you have meaningful connection with yourself, with others around you, and other beings, you don't really feel lonely. Wherever you go, you will always have company, you will be more at ease and settled, and people will be drawn to you more easily than when you are not. It is a very pleasant feeling that brings about contentment. It is happiness in its simplest form.

The contentment feeling I am referring to is not the same as just being complacent where we are not doing our best or striving to achieve our own level of personal excellence. Contentment here refs to the essence of a truly contented heart, it comes from a place of gratitude; of truly appreciating everything we have around us on a sincere level. If we just pause and consider for a moment, and think of all the things that we are grateful for, those are the moments that will allow us to feel even more happiness.

Too many times, we hear someone say, *"I'll be happy when I find my soul-mate, when I get married, or when I buy that beach house..."* Et cetera. These statements create a set of conditioning state, in our mind that prevent us from feeling *true happiness and contentment here and now.*

Accessing Happiness From Within

"Happiness begins with you. Inner peace and inner joy begins with you."

— *Linda Tomai Duong*

True contentment that brings about our ultimate happiness is the feeling that we want to attain, not the external and temporary happy emotions that come and go with elation in one moment and deflating the next. It is great to have financial success and/or a partner with whom to share your life, enjoyment, and achievements with; however, these are the *external layers* of happiness. *The finances we gain are outside of us. Our partners are also outside of us.*

When you look at happiness this way, you will be able to see that happiness is not a destination which you travel towards, or have to work hard to achieve. Neither can you wait for happiness to come from other people or sources, except to actually *feel the happiness, experience the happiness feeling, right here and right now.* By embracing the thought of accessing and reigniting the happiness we already have within us; we *will* immediately feel closer to happiness and true contentment.

Happiness is not a destination. Happiness can be accessed right here, right now. You can choose to access it; starting with the activation of your own connection.

— *Linda Tomai Duong*

Perspective of Happiness

"Practicing gratitude and being grateful for all there is every day, in everything we do, is a great way to access happiness from within!"
— *Linda Tomai Duong*

We all have a different vision of what happiness is and how it can be achieved, so we need to look at what our view and our perspective of happiness is.

What is your perspective of happiness? What do you need to achieve in order to be happy? It could be that you need to heal the world from diseases, hunger and poverty, get that doctorate degree, or be a multi-millionaire. And once achieved, what does it mean to you? And, do you have to achieve that goal before you can be happy? How about the incredible man with amazing inner strength; who had to drag himself on the floor to get to places, who needed a wheelchair but couldn't even have one – I wonder what his perspective of happiness is?

Whatever our perspective of happiness is attached to, we need to be mindful of anything that places too much drive or weight on the external factors, as that can become a kind of *conditioned* state of happiness, which happens when we place too much dependence on external circumstances and external sources.

While all the achievements can add to our happiness, it can also keep us too busy chasing the end goals and distracting us from appreciating the current achievements and enjoying the present moments. As a result it can prevent us from connecting with our inner-selves where the feelings of true contentment reside.

Imagine this, as a parent or carer, you may not like the activity of cleaning, but you know that a clean house will keep the place germ-free for the baby to crawl around, and that gives you the peace of mind to enjoy watching your baby crawling, which brings about those moments of inner joy. This kind of joy is not dependent on the outside sources but is felt from within, and is based on the choice you have made.

Therefore, the choices we make, the attachments we create towards our perspective of happiness are what we need to have clarity of, so that we can achieve happiness more in our everyday life.

We can choose to work towards something that will result in happiness which comes from inner joy and inner-peace, those that come from the momentary feeling of being happy and from the outside sources, or those from instant gratification which misled us to be happiness but could actually bring us pain in the end, instead of happiness.

Some activities such as addictive gaming, gambling, or taking substances and other adulterous activities that may provide instant gratification, short-term excitement, and/or a the instant state of ecstasy, but often lack deeper meaning and inner peace, and over time erode our self-contentment rather leading us to attaining contentment. We need to see the differences between these in order to gain the clarity. Otherwise it can blind us to the future consequences that lead us to feelings of deflation, loss and depression. Or worse, getting us into a vicious cycle whereby we don't want to feel unhappy and so we seek that instant gratification again, only to quickly lose that momentary thrill and fall back into a low mood, causing the depressive feelings and creating an unhealthy pattern perpetually. It is a pattern that causes the need to continue the unwanted cycle of craving the elusive feeling of being 'happy', which actually takes away, rather than increases our true happiness – the inner joy and inner peace.

When we find meanings in what we do, that is when we feel a deeper gratitude and true contentment. Such as, someone dreams of owning a beach house, not because of the expensive location or status but because they can be closer to the sea nature and be closer to marine animals, which gives them the connection they craved, and in turn, brings them their joy and happiness. That is what gives them meaning to work hard to pay for the mortgage, and all the while enjoy feeling contented. Such individuals tend to be more motivated and content due to their deeper gratitude for the things in their life.

It is our perspective and attachment of happiness that gives us the meaning and drive; to do what we do in achieving our happiness. Once we have formed a certain view and become attached to that view, we would go above and beyond to achieve the vision that we have formed in our minds. This brings us the kind of contentment that may not always be related to financial success or fame. The fame or amount of money earned for its own sake does not have the ability to bring true contentment and happiness from within, unless it has meaning attached to it. Therefore, it is a must in having this clarity between achieving happiness from inner peace, or happiness that is dependent on outside sources, when we think about our perspective of happiness.

Some people in some parts of the world are grateful to have the basics of food, shelter, and to feel safe. Having these basics met were enough for them to access their happiness. Others must a lot more or be a millionaire before they will say that they have achieved happiness.

Whatever your perspective, definition and connection to happiness is, having clarity on how you connect your definition of happiness and your value, satisfaction, and expectations, together with the acceptance of your situation, is what brings about equanimity.

Positivity and Generosity Increases Happiness

We all know that with positivity in life, we can achieve happiness more often. The practice of being positive or having an optimistic attitude in life can bring about happiness faster than any other way. For example, see the below conversation that I have witnessed at the end of a leadership seminar:

Jacinta: "So, what's your take away?"

Lily: "The confirmation that I have the same leadership skills."

Jacinta: "So you just wasted $500.00, came all the way here, and got nothing out of it."

Lily: "Or I can say, how amazing it is to know that I can be such a leader too, if I chose, as it has now confirmed that I have those same qualities."

Lily could have chosen to feel unhappy that she had spent $500.00 and wasted her time to learn nothing new. Or she could choose to see the benefits in boosting her confidence, knowing that she now has the confirmation she needed, which was why she went there to begin with. By choosing the positive view, she was immediately happier and can boost her self-belief and confidence as well, rather than feeling unhappy that she had spent the investment with no returns.

From the above conversation, it has emphasised to me even more that our perspective of happiness is not only in the subject matter itself, as in which activity we associate happiness with, but also from which perspective or which angle we choose to see things so that we can maintain our happiness.

When I think of perspectives of happiness, it brings me back to the memory of my great first models in life. I recall on numerous occasions when others had turned to my parents for financial support and asked to borrow money; even though they were struggling to look after a family of 12 themselves, they still helped whenever they could. In some cases, they lent as much as they had, ignoring their own hardship, knowing that others were more desperate for help. I put that down to their positive attitudes as they often said: "No matter what happens, things will work out" and it was with that attitude they carried, that things really did always work out.

One particular incident has stayed with me since eight years of age. We were doing slightly better financially, and by now, my mum and dad were busy running a corner shop. The eldest child and the youngest child have an age gap of 20 years in my family. While two of older siblings were into their adulthood and trying out, testing their business trading skills, I was growing well, starting to feel confident and was able to ride a bike confidently to the local market and places within in the district area, and often rode to the market to buy things on my own.

One day, my brother came home excitedly as he had bargained his very first good deal and bought a brand new bike for the girls in the family; there were five boys and five girls. The bike looked very attractive with fresh metallic-pink paint and new wheels. I was eager to test it out. Coincidentally, the cook in the family, which is the fifth sister, had asked me to go and get shallots for her, as she had forgotten them when she was buying her ingredients at the market.

As soon as I got to the market, a bald-headed, skinny and pregnant lady waved at me. She had my attention. I looked at her flimsy frame and felt for her. I went over to her and she said quietly. "You have these gold stud earrings showing, you better follow me and take this quiet path so that you're not so easily seen." It was if I was hypnotised or something; somehow, I just followed her quietly.

I was a quiet girl and so her soft and gentle voice didn't feel like a threat to me. As I stood right next to her, I also sensed her desperate emotions, it spoke to the compassionate side of me, and with all my guards down I actually believed her. I trusted her. I didn't think she was going to do any harm to me. She then said: "Actually, you'd better let me keep those gold earrings safe for you." And without caring for an answer, she just reached over to my ears and took them off. I must have fallen under her spell because I let her remove my earrings and stayed quiet. I still can remember the images clearly.

By nature, I was very quiet and obliging. I was aware that there were tricksters and pickpockets. However, with her skinny and pregnant frame, she looked harmless to me. I sensed her anxiousness, I felt for her, and I followed her diligently and quietly. Somehow, she convinced me that I should let her double me on my brand new bike; I don't remember saying a word to reject any of her suggestions. I really must have been hypnotised. I simply did as I was told.

After a short while, we ended up at a beautiful church with a very open and large space outside. I thought I was in a different city or something. I had only been around my own area and had only seen Buddhist temples and they were mostly very old. Whereas the outside of this building looked new and beautiful. I was then, instructed to squat behind the bell tower and "Do not come out. Shhh...!" Again, in my hypnotised state, I did as I was told, and all the while I felt her anxiety. The feeling that you know something is not right and yet you want to believe that everything is okay started to emerge.

I waited, waited, and waited some more... after sometime, it was almost as if the hypnotism had worn off. I was slowly coming back to my alert state and started using my logical mind again, and thought "Hold on, I have been squatting here, hiding for some time now, what am I hiding from? Where is the bald-headed, skinny and pregnant lady? And where is this place? And how come there is no one else here? I think it's time to leave and go home."

I walked out on to the street as my old clever-self came back, and I waved a Xích Lô — the Vietnamese rickshaw in a very calm and collected manner, in fact with some level of quiet confidence and told the man my address for him to take me home. I did not show any signs of distress or that I was scared or nervous. I also remembered to keep a calm face and did not let my anxiousness show, even though I was very anxious to get home.

It turns out that I was in another district, which luckily wasn't that far away. The whole experience was quite bizarre, considering that at the beginning, I was literally a puppet following this desperate, bald-headed and pregnant woman, where I did not do much thinking as if she blinded me to trust her and obey her every instruction. Yet, after the 'waking' state, I became quite clever and confident in calling for the Xích Lô and had the rider respect my instructions and take me home. I mean, who would take instruction from an eight-year-old child back then? Thinking back, it was a bit spellbinding in a way as I did not feel endangered or scared at all.

Upon arriving home, my brother and my mum looked at me in surprise as I got off the Xích Lô "Where's the new bike?" they asked me. Of course, I didn't even have to answer and they knew what had happened. Life was basic but tough, and a constant struggle for all. Pickpockets were common, and many people had to ignore their conscience and block their guilt and shame in the struggle to make a living. The focus was on functioning and surviving. I don't remember hearing complicated news like murder or violent charges. It was mainly all about small thieves struggling for their daily survival.

Looking back, what surprised me more was the attribute about my parents, which had led me to keep this memory; they were never cynical about things. They did not say one negative word about this incident. The stolen studs were my very first pair of tiny gold studs and were so precious. They didn't even scold me for losing them nor did they show disappointment that I lost the new bike. All they said was: "Oh, you fell for their trap!" In fact, my mum said it with a chuckle. And it didn't even bother my dad. And since they both were calm, my brother reacted calmly too.

He wasn't even upset at me. Nobody was really upset as they all had one common understanding. The lady was desperate and needed my golden earrings and bike to exchange for money to support her upcoming newborn.

This incident taught me so much about life ahead. Instead of looking at what we have lost, my parents' compassion and generosity had taught me to be kind even in situations when you think you can't be. They had taught me that we are here for each other, in one way or another. We serve each other and we are all linked somehow to lean on each other.

Never did they even say one negative word about this incident. Not even suggesting that I should be more clever next time or anything like that. Their outlook on life was always in harmony, even though they did argue among themselves. I mean, which marriage doesn't involve arguments? Especially when you have 12 mouths to feed. Yet, with such amount of responsibility, they somehow still, always managed to see the positive side of life.

Instead of being upset at the loss of my gold earrings and new bike, my parents saw the benefits that the woman gained. Instead of viewing the incident as me being tricked, they viewed it as a life lesson for me. They somehow always managed to take the positive viewpoint of life. They only made one comment, that I fell for the trap and that was it. They did not waste any energy at all in talking about the negative side of this incident. We *never* talked about it again. Had they panicked about the incident and dwelled on the loss of the gold earrings and the new bike, those responses would have turned me into a very different person than I am today. Imagine if they had scolded and yelled at me and made comments such as I should have been smarter rather than being tricked. What do you think that would have made me feel?

I could have turned out to be a very anxious person and wary of being tricked again. I might not have trusted anyone from then on and lived my life in a state of anxiety each time I went out to see the world. That would *not only* have affected my self-esteem and self-confidence, with the belief and self-image that I was not smart enough to avoid the trap, when we all clearly know it was a set up. It would have also crippled me for life.

The way my parents modelled their outlook on life inspired me to live with trust instead of fear. To choose the positive instead of the negative. To be compassionate and generous instead of being self-centred;

I have learned:

To trust that we all can care for each other and that things happen only out of situational desperation.

That we can always choose to look at the positive side of things in life. Choosing to be positive in life frees us from our own prison of worry and sorrow.

To give generously from the heart — when we open our hearts to each other, we accept that there are challenges in life, and we meet these challenges with humility, patience and compassion. With this understanding, we open ourselves fully to life with love and meaningful relationships with each other.

This childhood experience and the learning from it has also inspired me to have the insight into how to bring our children up in a carefree way, so that they feel empowered rather than living with feelings of fear and anxiety.

One of the ways I can think of is to practice and operate from the place of abundance in our minds and hearts. Feel from the place of abundance even when you have little. This is what I see my parents practiced and modelled for me. We weren't rich, but we obviously had enough for the lady to target me and take advantage of our resources, to help her out of her desperate situation. My parents' attitude showed me that if we operate from the place of abundance, from the generosity of the heart, we are more relaxed about the issues in life and can turn our minds to the positive aspects than if we were to operate from the place of scarcity, which tends to brings about negativity, worry and stress.

When we think that we are okay, and that we can make do with what we have, we tend to be more creative, which brings about positivity. Once in a positive mind-frame, we become creative, and creativity is what brings about even more positivity. It is an upward spiral thinking pattern. Instead of such thoughts as: "I am not okay and I don't have what I need to achieve what I want," or "I don't feel good enough" et cetera, et cetera, which quickly brings us into a downward spiral thinking pattern.

As you can see, *it is inevitable that only when we are being positive that we can experience joy and happiness.*

TIPS FOR FUN:

Challenge yourself to see if you can turn any negative situation into a positive one.

Here are some small everyday examples:

I don't like rainy weather, but it's good for the farmers and my garden.

I don't like hot, sunny days, but it gives us Vitamin D, which is good for my bones and teeth.

I hate traffic jams, but it slows you down so that you can process all that is happening around you.

The train door closes just as you walk up, but now you have a chance to grab your much-needed morning coffee before you start your working day.

Someone knocks over your cup of coffee! It gives you a chance to practice compassion and forgiveness as it was an innocent accident.

Now it's your turn to come up with situations that you can turn into a more positive outlook on life.

Being Positive is a Choice

When we think that we can't do anything about a given situation, we will find that we simply can't. It is because we have already predetermined the outcome. We have given up on the situation as our mind has already stopped finding positive and possible solutions. We simply have told our mind "Don't bother!" and it stops looking for solutions.

On the other hand, positive thoughts can have more powers than we think. When we keep hope and faith, and believe that "If there's a will, there's a way" our minds won't stop until it finds a solution. Creativity comes in and that brings about all the possibilities. This brings me to the memories and examples of how the people survived war times.

Creativity breeds possibility, which drives positive actions and positive outcomes. As soon as our mind thinks positively, our creative power comes in, and it might even come in ways that surprise you. Just by simply asking yourself: "How else can I do this?" or "How would the wiser me do this?" Your brain will naturally go searching for ways to deal with the situation and won't stop until it finds the best possible way to achieve a solution for the given situation. Once you can do it *habitually*, you will see that with positive thinking, you are more optimistic and are happier and healthier, allowing you to enjoy more success. You will also connect with others more positively. When we think we can always do something about any given situation, we can in fact have a positive effect on *any given situation.* This is because our positive thinking ignites creative ideas that we may not have thought of before we had to face the challenges. Our brain can switch its ingenuity on and provide a creative solution for every challenge it is presented.

"It is inevitable that only when we are being positive that we can experience joy and happiness."

Linda Tomai Duong

Chapter 4

Happiness in Self-Connection

Recognising that you can access happiness immediately, will give you the power to claim it within yourself, here and now!"

— Linda Tomai Duong

The Self-Connection Journey

I have discovered that being alone and loneliness are two different things. We could be in a room full of people and yet feel lonely. Other times, we can be in a room with no one but never feel lonely. This is because when we feel connected with ourselves and others, we also are aware and feel connected with our surroundings, and all other beings, allowing us to feel the companies around us. Hence we don't feel lonely.

Once you can connect with yourself by tuning in, being aware of your own feelings and emotions, and being able to acknowledge and express how you truly feel in a sensible and respectful manner, you will be able to express your true feelings authentically in a way that makes people feel attracted to you. As a result, they are more incline to want to help you if you need help, and want to be connected to you. You will find that, over time, it is easier to articulate your feelings to others without such feeling as being needy or self-pity. Not only that, you will also gaining compassion and respect at the same time, which are all the feelings that contribute to feeling at peace.

In contrast, when we lack self-connection, we don't feel comfortable "in our own skin," and making it difficult to begin conversations with others and to be able to connect with others comfortably and easily. This results in us feeling lonely, even when there are many people present in the same room.

Being aware and acknowledging our own feelings and emotions is the first step to self-connection. For example, if you are feeling happy, it is easy to know what to do. But, what about when you feel lonely or upset, disrespected, cheated, or in between? How do you deal with that? Would you like to talk to someone or prefer solitary time? Would you prefer to write your feelings down, do boxing or some other physical exercise? Or listen to music, go dancing, swimming, running, jogging or would you prefer a walk in nature, perhaps a walk by the beach? Or read a book to escape into another world?

Whichever way you choose to deal with the unsettling emotions, let it all out in a healthy way so that you can regain balance and feel settled again.

Connect to Yourself and to Your Intuitive Voice

Once we feel settled with our emotions and have clarity in our heads, we can feel the space and calmness in our minds. That is when we are able to tune in and hear our intuitive voice.

My first experience of hearing my own intuitive voice was when I was about 12 years old. Back then, gas and electric stoves were not used in the average household. Most of the households used firewood for cooking. By then, my dad had moved on from having the corner shop to selling firewood. In one incident, I was able to listen to my intuitive voice and that was what guided and protected me from a possible head and facial injury.

Imagine this; the wooden logs were split vertically into narrower pieces to suit small wood fire stoves. They were then bundled up into small bundles with a vine right in the middle to be sold as individual bundles. Due to the vines being in the middle of the firewood length, it created unevenness and instability when stacked up against the wall, and without frames to support them, the piles could fall easily when stacked too high.

That day, the wall of split firewood was almost as high as the ceiling, and as I was about to walk past that wall of split firewood,

I heard a voice say: "Bigger step!" It was quiet but clear, firm and warm all at the same time. Instinctively, I leapt, and the second that my feet landed on the other side of the step, the whole wall of firewood collapsed right behind me. I can still hear that same voice in my mind as I write this, just as I heard it years ago. This experience has taught me to tune in and connect with myself more than ever, since that day.

An example image of the logs being split for home cooking.

Home cooking stoves in Vietnam.

Tune Out to Tune In

When you have a pressing, personal, or big philosophical question, and you really want to have an answer for it, try to be patient and give yourself time, rather than let it frustrate you with the urge to seek out the answer. Be patient and allow yourself some time and find a quiet place so that you can be on your own to contemplate your questions.

This process is most effective if you're outdoors in nature. Whether it is by the beach, a lake, a mountain, a garden or park, anywhere outside with fresh air will help you to relax and tune into your intuitive thoughts and feelings better. You also need to be able to be alone so that you are not distracted. Even if you have companies, you just need to sit and relax by yourself. With the fresh air, take a few conscious breaths, and allow yourself to feel your surroundings. Listen to the nearby water, whisper of the wind or any other sounds like birds et cetera. Take in nature's beauty.

Once you are all settled and somewhat relaxed you can ask yourself those mind bothering questions, and take it slow and easy. One thought or question at a time. I call this process *tuning in*. You are connecting with nature to connect with yourself. You are turning inward rather than seeking outward to get the answers you are seeking. If you stay quiet and really get in touch with yourself, with your thoughts deeply but in a relaxing way, hence being in the outdoor and in nature helps. This is how you connect with your higher-self. It simply means that you tune out of your busy daily life, leave your worrisome thoughts behind and tune in to your pure thoughts – thoughts that bring out your full potential, it holds no fear and no judgments, it speaks freely to you and sees no boundary except from the place of highest, and deepest wisdom that you don't get to uncover due to the daily busyness. This is how and why you will most likely find the answers you're looking, or at least options to look at the questions with a different and fresh viewpoint. At the end of this process, you will feel much more settled, relaxed, and lighter. Most of the time it feels peaceful to me during and at the end of the process. All by myself – undisturbed. Once you get used to it, you will enjoy the serenity and connectedness that you feel, and that's the ultimate feeling of this process.

I have taught my two children to tune in whenever they need to from the age of six and eight. I say to them, if you're away from mummy and you feel upset, you can talk to a trusted adult or, you can ask yourself: "If I ask mummy about this question, what would mummy say or advise me to do?" Or "If you feel upset and you don't want to talk to anybody, then ask your bigger-self, for advice on what to do." And "If you're really upset and need comforting but mummy is not there, then comfort your younger-self and say, 'It's okay. You can cry.' And let yourself have a good cry." This is how we can teach our children to tune in to themselves. Like many beneficial things, it's a good habit for children to learn early at their appropriate age level.

It all starts with us igniting that connection we have within ourselves and beginning to have connection to our own depth of thoughts and emotions, then, we can connect with others, nature and all beings. Ultimately, the universe at large, and that is when see deeper meanings in life.

"Connection is always what keeps our souls alive and provides the answers that we are seeking."

- Linda Tomai Duong.

Eventually, with practice, you can get to a place where you feel content and happy with the simplest things in life. Appreciating all beings, feeling peace and settled that you can smile from the inside out and do it without intentional awareness. Has that happened to you? When you are thinking happy thoughts and did not realise you were actually smiling...? That is happiness from the inside out.

Others don't need to know what you're smiling about, only you know what makes you smile. This is when your happiness is on the highest level and the vibration of your energy can be passed on to others and they can actually feel it from you, even without you telling them you are feeling happy.

This is when you are in your true happiness state. A state where your genuine happiness energy spreads wherever you go. People around you will love your presence wherever you go. As you enter a room, your uplifting mood brings about the positive vibe and energy that radiates and spreads out and gets transmitted to those who are present in the room without them even noticing. That is the magic happiness brings when everyone gets cheered up but no one knows why. Not even you. You will simply feel warm, welcoming, elated and glad that you came into the room.

True contentment and happiness is what ignites our hearts and souls. It really allows us to truly feel *alive and awakened,* feeling satisfied from the inside out is the kind of feeling that lasts, not the surface feelings and emotions that pass through us and fluctuate, depended upon our external circumstances.

"We need to turn inwards and tune into ourselves in order to access our strength and happiness."

— Linda Tomai Duong

Connection and Gratitude

When we are calm and can tune in, we can feel and experience inner peace and inner joy more often, which is completely different to those *"external layers of happiness"*. From my experience, I have learned that by tuning in, we also begin to activate and experience the feelings of gratitude that we otherwise are too busy to think of or feel.

As I was growing up, being aware of my surroundings, I also started to be aware and saw wider views in my own community in Vietnam, and developed more empathy, appreciation, and gratitude for what we already have, rather than wishing for what we don't have. Having gratitude for those who don't have full health and yet were *still* able to achieve what some might think of as unachievable.

I have witnessed these incredible *"differently-abled"* individuals who didn't even have wheel-chairs due to the limited resources time and place that we lived in at the time, and yet they still managed and carried on with hope and faithful spirits. They have demonstrated unstoppable willpower. Whether they lack arms or had no legs, it didn't matter. Nothing stopped them from accessing their amazing inner strength. It was apparent that their unshakable emotional and mental state to earn a living and to continue on with life comes from a place of spiritual strength that required peace from within; in order for them to access that deep level of resilience to go on — and to say that I absolutely admired these incredible individuals is an understatement. They inspired me to develop more inner strength in myself.

When we create more meaningful connections, develop more grateful thought patterns, and regularly practice expressing the feelings of reverence for the things we have been given then we will naturally begin to feel more joy and will naturally spread joy to others too. These days, many of us spend days thinking about what we want now and what we want next. It is often not until certain times such as Thanksgiving, or similar occasions that we are reminded to think about what we are grateful for and how to express that gratitude.

Practicing gratitude and being grateful for all that we have in everyday life and in everything we do; be it something very basic, like being able to walk - such a very simple yet essential thing in life that we take for granted. Or other things such as education, clean water and a job that enables us to provide for our family, et cetera, is a great way to access happiness from within, and when we do that we tend to have a more positive outlook on life, which again leads us to feel happiness more easily and frequently, which is a very uplifting cycle of emotions to have.

Happiness in Self-Love

"Happiness is here. Access your happiness right here, right now."

— Linda Tomai Duong

As we talk about self-love, I would like to invite you to take a breather and travel the down memory lane to relive some good, old memories, to ignite some of the positive feelings and to feel refreshed. To find more inner joy and to nurture more self-love.

Do you remember what it felt like when you first had a crush on someone? Remember those exciting feelings you had on that first date? When you finally found someone that you could call your boyfriend, girlfriend or your soulmate? If you remember, it is like nothing else on earth matters during those moments. Feelings such as "Love conquers all!" If he says: "Let's climb the mountain", you climb the mountain. If she says: "Let's move to the beach", you move to beach; that kind of devoted feeling is what I'm referring to - the feelings of deep intimate emotional connections, excitements, and passions. All of those loving feelings and emotions can bring back our life-force, putting us back into the 'driver's' mode.

When we are in love, everything seems so perfect. We are full of live and there is this invisible driving force that empowers us to conquer the world if we must, to be with love and be with our loved one. Our hearts are burning with desire and feeling beautiful from the inside out or at least most of the time, anyway. This is when we sing, "*Love is in the air!*" And even when it isn't perfect, or not all beautiful, we still turn up to try and do things with the other person, mostly *for* the other person, and try to make things work, or fix it, and do whatever that love requires us to do.

These are the moments in life that we are most motivated and most engaged. This is when we are most diligent in what we do, we do our best to impress, to achieve more, to accomplish more, and mainly to show a good, high standard to reflect back on who we really are and what we are capable of. In the end, it is all because we are *in love*. And we want to be the best for the other person and us, not just for ourselves. Sometimes, this applies to being a parent too; being and doing our best for our children. They are our invisible driving force that give us the power to go on, even when we think we can't.

This is the state of feeling you want to get back to. To be feeling that you are doing your best, to engage with yourself with the passions you now have just elicited. Keep this feeling as you continue on. However, this time it is not necessarily about being with another person. You are no longer doing your best for someone else but *for yourself*. Applying this same drive and same passion you have for your "new love" — yourself. This is how you can reclaim your self-love. Self-love is what allows you to reconnect with our own self more deeply.

Most of us operate from a selfless stance. Caring for others is much easier. It makes us feel important and wanted; it gives us meaning in life. However, we also need to realise that we will be able to care for others even more when we regain or have more self-love.

This is *when* you can experience happiness, satisfaction and contentment again if you feel that you have lost it. Because you now have rediscovered your self-love.

When you embrace this journey of reclaiming your self-love and self-connection, *you will rediscover the invisible driving force within you, and it all stems from self-love.*

"Self-love is infinite love. We must have self-love before we can love others."

— Linda Tomai Duong

83

Happiness in Self-Worth

"We need to feel self-worth to access happiness."

— *Linda Tomai Duong*

Having self-love we naturally take better self-care which is what we deserve. Sometimes we forget to allow ourselves the self-love to come first, which is relating to self-worth. Certain views or expectations that we have been brought up with, may have influenced our judgment of our self-value and self-worth, and that is why we sometimes we put our self-love last.

Views such as: "Men shouldn't cry and if they do, they are weak". Or, in some cultures, when women are menstruating, they are seen as "dirty" and don't get the same treatment and respect as they normally would during other days of the month. Such misconceptions affect the way we see ourselves and impact the way we value ourselves.

There are many other views and perspectives that had been passed on from the previous generations with different cultural values. Having been born in the Eastern cultures and growing up in the Western world, I have come to learn and become aware that some of the ancient wisdoms are invaluable and that, they should be passed on for generations to come as I have shared a few of the valuable wisdoms in the earlier chapters. Of course, by the same token, some 'old-wives' tales' can be abolished when they no longer serve us.

As young children, we cannot help but to accept what gets passed on to us by our parents, grandparents, and care givers. We literally just absorb and model everything we see and learn. However, as adults now, we have the knowledge and ability to analyse, reflect and make our own judgments about what we have been told, and can be critical about the views we adopt. I am by no means advocating for rebellious manners. But my intention is to suggest that we can even at times, with appropriateness and respect, challenge those old ways of thinking by asking ourselves the following critical questions:

Where did those ideas, habits or customs derive from?

What do those views or perspectives really mean?

What purpose or value does that view point or perspective serve me now as an adult, living and functioning as a global citizen?

How do these views help me grow as a person?

By embracing these views or old teachings, will they hinder me from moving forward, or will they help me grow?

How do these views, or perspectives serve me in forming my self-value? And the values that I will pass on to the generations to come?

Ever since the ancient times, we look up to our elders because they have been on the path before us and can share their insights, triumphs and tribulations with us, to save us from repeating the same mistakes and pain, and to make life easier for us. We gain from their wisdom and their experiences, yet we must also remember that some of the old-wives' tales were formulated out of restrictive environments, with limited resources and limited education. Therefore, we must be aware of the difference between wisdom that are good to learn from, as opposed to the old-wives' tales that no longer serve us. This means that we must apply some level of critical thinking to form better decisions about whether or not to accept those learnings. For example, one of the Eastern culture's old-wives' tales is that new mothers should NOT bathe or wash their hair for the first 100 days after the baby is born. She should also rest, keep warm and stay still and have someone else nurse her during this period. What do you think about this old-wives' tale?

For a start, I wouldn't mind having someone to nurse me for the first 100 days of being a new mother, but I am not sure if I could stand not washing myself and my hair for 100 days. It would be quite unhygienic, don't you think? So, of course I didn't follow that advice. But as time went by, I have found out that many others who were born or live in Australia with a Chinese cultural background still follow that tradition. They may have a shower but they do not wash their hair for 100 days. Now, given the climate in most parts of Australia, we do mostly have air conditioning so it might be bearable, but it did pique my curiosity to try and understand more.

I have learned from physiotherapists, that Asian people's bones are more flexible and that this is in our genes. No wonder that Asian people can squat so easily. I was also advised by the Chinese herbalist and doctor that a new mother's body loosens up all over during pregnancy and child-birth, including even our pores. Women expand continuously during pregnancy, making us all "loose and fragile" as we make room inside for the baby to grow. The 100 days' rest or doing minimal work allows us to heal our body back to its pre-pregnancy form, or as close to it as possible. During this period, it is believed that if we bathe or shower, the water can get in to our bones through the opened pores, which can cause arthritis in old age. I learned this information a few years after my children were born, so if I was to do it again, of course having someone to nurse me for the first 100 days would be fantastic! Although I would balance out the hygiene concerns with the possible cause of future arthritis in old age... The point I am sharing is that we must investigate and evaluate some of the beliefs that have been passed down to us and balance this knowledge with our current situation rather than listen "blindly" and feel obliged to follow, or discount them all together when there could be invaluable benefits and lessons behind a belief. This applies to all different cultures.

Through this *belief-evaluation* process, I call it, we can become more in tune with our thoughts, and gain more knowledge about life in general, and be more self-empowered rather than being governed by some outdated values or be obliged to the rules that can impede us from achieving our happiness and inner peace.

Definition: Belief-evaluation means to assess and balance out the knowledge of a belief, with our current situation rather than listen "blindly" and feel obliged to follow, or discount them all together when there could be invaluable benefits and lessons behind a belief.

— *Linda Tomai Duong*

This belief evaluation process not only increases our confidence as an individual but also leads us to become more engaged in our lives, in our environment, and in the community we live in. It is this curiosity, engagement and lifelong learning that will also leads us to think deeply about our values in general, our self-value, which essentially guides us back to self-worth.

We need to see the value of ourselves in order to have deeper self-love and then be able to love others more deeply. When we lack self-worth and self-love, it is difficult for us to feel loved by others. No matter how much they try to show us their love, we cannot feel it, or we may not feel deserving of their love and cannot enjoy the love that is coming our way. If we feel unworthy of love, we tend to neglect self-care and start to disconnect from ourselves, which is the opposite of what we want — self-connection. Self-connection is what will lead us back to self-worth and self-love.

TIPS:

Avoid Distractions to Tune into Yourself

"Happiness is already inside you. Avoid external distractions so that you can tune into your inner-self to access your happiness."

— Linda Tomai Duong

As we all know, being in the present moment is definitely the key to access happiness. However, let's look at why it is so difficult for us to be in the present moment and why it is a challenge these days to stay connected. There are two primary interferences that keep our minds from being present and prevent us from staying connected with ourselves and with others.

TIP 1

Distractions from Technology

Apart from our already busy minds, there's the busyness of the modern world of technology with emails, the internet, television, iPhones, social media and computer games overloading our minds on a daily basis. So, at times we need to detach from this external world to return to our internal world in order to recharge, and be able to reattach again with new and refreshed energy. In other words, we need to allow ourselves downtime from the external word to have more quiet times to nurture ourselves, to replenish and recharge before we can continue our journey in a healthy way.

As we are constantly checking our phones for messages and for email updates, it's is evident that we are actually craving connections with others. We are constantly wanting to see the messages and can't wait to reply to them the minute one comes through.

The trouble with connecting randomly like this throughout the day is that it can create too many distractions and frequent disruptions to our work routine and it certainly does not encourage the concentration and focus required to nurture quality work and quality relationships. It is much better to have dedicated times to connect properly. Putting our phone on silent mode, or turning mobile phone notifications off during work hours will enable us to focus on specific tasks, which is the key to being present to be efficient, effective, and satisfied with ourselves and our performance, which in turn allows us to feel satisfied, happy, and content, that we have enjoyed a productive day in the end.

It is also important to be aware of how we use the time, technology, and the connections so that it becomes meaningful, whether it is for work or for personal purposes, and keeping in mind our intentions and actions while engaging in online activities will also benefit our wellbeing. By allocating a dedicated timeslot to online activities such as social media, it can help us greatly to focus and mitigate the 'invisible' distraction throughout the day.

TIP 2:

Worrying Thoughts

"Worry robs our feelings of joy. Never worry."

— Linda Tomai Duong

Another factor that keeps our minds overly busy and distracted is the tendency to worry. When we lend to the thought of 'what if' too much, it results in us being absentminded, anxious, unnecessarily worried, and living in anticipation of impending problems.

The moment we begin to have worrying thoughts, it is difficult for us to have our minds present. Worrying and anxiety is a complex issue, and I would leave that to the psychologists. Here, my focus is to only try to address it briefly, to remind us the importance of being in the present moment. As soon as our minds start to think about any concerning thoughts, immediately it preoccupies our mind and takes us away from being present.

This is not to say that we cannot think about things we are genuinely concerned about but it is important to do it in an intentional way. For example, looking out the window at work and thinking: "Oh it's rainy! The clothes are out hanging on the clothes line and they're getting all wet!" This is a perfectly natural response with rational thought, and you can actively choose to problem solve in a counterproductive way such as: "Oh well, the worst is that they will all get wet and I'll just have to wash them again or put them into the dryer when I get home". Once this concerning thought is addressed, you can literally 'park' the matter and free up your mind to go back to the task at hand.

Unfortunately, there are times when we allow our worrying thoughts go loose and out of control. For example: "Oh it's rainy! The clothes are out hanging on the clothes line and they're getting all wet! I think the kids' school uniforms are out there and if they are then it will be really bad, because I won't have time to rewash them and they can't go in the dryer and... oh no! I won't even be able to do that as there's just so much going on tonight!" Etc., Etc. And we end up being distracted, preoccupied without us realising it. Worst, before we know it, our thoughts go into a downward spiral pattern adding more worry and anxiety with absolutely non-productive thoughts, and suddenly it is impossible for us to bring our minds back to the present moment. It is also very draining once this thought pattern starts, which takes away our energy to connect with our love ones. Hence, being aware of how we think can help us bring our minds back into the present moment, and we need to catch these thoughts early to keep them under control.

Recently I was at the butchers and a male employee greeted me: "How are you doing?" to which I replied, "Ok", appreciating that he took a moment to ask and connect, but the conversation continued on like this:

Him: "I'll feel better if the rain stops. It's been raining all week! I need the sun to dry my washing! You know…"

Me: "I see, how about you put it in a dryer?"

Him: "No, I don't have a dryer."

Me: "Oh I see, how about you put them on a rack next to the heater?"

Him: "No, I don't have a heater and that costs too much electricity!"

Me: "I see, how about you iron them first then use a hair dryer to blow dry them afterwards?"

Him: "Or I'll put them on rack and put it over my car engine!"

The above conversation shows how the young man started with a negative frame of mind but because his concerns had been voiced aloud and acknowledged, he was able to come up with a creative solution in the end.

As exaggerated as it sounds, sometimes it is creativity that causes people to magnify their worries. I call this *Negative-Creative thinking*. When Negative-Creative thinking. The key here is to 'catch' those moments that we are about to 'indulge' in negative-creative thinking and to mentally park it aside and know that you can revisit it during the *intentional thinking* time slot that you have allocated. This is taking a proactive approach rather than reacting to the urge that surfaces.

Definition: Negative-Creative thinking is when people use their creativity and apply the creative thoughts in a negative thought pattern to magnify their worries and concerns around a situation, and it is often done at the wrong time without realising that they are doing so.

— Linda Tomai Duong

Indulging in negative-creative thought patterns really keep us distracted and pre-occupied. It often causes a downward spiral thought pattern, which is debilitating, as the process can drain our energy, which can be used for far more productive and positive activities. It is much better to allocate intentional, and creative thinking time, which is far healthier and productive then the mind using its creativity at the wrong time. This is especially seen in bright children, whom need to be allowed a lot of creative time during the day and throughout their early growing years to help nurture their creative minds and to avoid them turning their creative ideas in to mischievous behaviours.

A simple and effective strategy to manage negative-creative thinking, is to do "active thinking" with some sorting and reflective thinking involved. By setting aside a time, it could be daily, weekly, or monthly, depending on your own need. It could be done either in the morning or at night;

Write out all the things that you currently have on your mind or need to attend to.

Write down any concerns or worries so that you can pro-actively plan for them with actionable steps.

Then, plan in advance a time in your day to actively attend to them, rather than waiting until things happen and then having to react to them.

Have some time for creative thinking and new ideas to surface.

The intent is to simply reflect on what has worked and what hasn't in order to plan for better future actions, also, so that you can ease away any bothering thoughts by actively acknowledge them. Usually the act of acknowledging the worrying thought consciously and even aloud, will provide us with clarity around the issue to free up our mind. By attending to concerns proactively and creating time creative ideas to surface, we won't have to use negative-creative thinking.

It is good to have a habit of catching the negative-creative thoughts early and challenge them, by asking ourselves "What is the worst that could happen?" Then replace them with positive thought patterns and an actionable step to lead to a more positive outcome. As it helps to clear our minds regularly.

Like a child, our minds are active and hungry for attention and stimulation. It needs creative time and needs to be 'fed'. If you feed it good information, it will give you good productive thoughts, such as learning new things, meeting new people and connecting with old friends, or joining group activities. If we ignore the brain's need, we will have it bother us like a child does, when they come and grab you by your leg until you give them attention, just like those times when the brain starts with those negative 'what if' chain of thoughts, and often keep you up at night. Therefore, it is much healthier to allocate playtime or 'distraction time' as well as intentional thinking, and planning time. Apart from these, studying something to gain new knowledge or learning a new hobby are a great ways to keep our mind stimulated, entertained and satisfied.

Another way to reduce anxious thoughts so that we can be more present, is to limit your exposure to the bad news that seems to be prevalent these days; just skim through it to be aware of what's going on in the world if you must, but be selective of the kind of news you watch and follow, so that your mind won't be disturbed too much by all the negativity going on. Once we get emotionally attached, negative thoughts and heavy emotions can come in and we start to lose faith, lose trust and doubt our own safety and security.

Whenever we watch the news at home, we need to be mindful too, that we turn off the TV when it gets too disheartening, especially if there are young children present. Children don't need to know about all the bad news in the world. They just need to understand about safety, how to stay safe and be alert. They also need to learn positive knowledge that helps them grow in an informed way — not to grow up with negative news and negative messages around them.

Children who watch too much bad news can be impacted more negatively than what we are aware of. It may give them the message that the world is not a safe place. The last thing we want is for our children to grow up feeling constantly anxious and worried about their safety as they go about their daily lives. Worry takes away our freedom to feel joy. If we worry all the time, how can we possibly feel happiness?

TIP 3:

From Worry to Acceptance to Peace Within

Apart from lessening the worry, we need to be able to have acceptance in order to have peace and happiness from within. When we discuss about being worried and being at peace, we often think of adults only. Here, I would like to bring our attention to children as well, so that we can help them access happiness and peace as they grow – that is my wish for the future generations. We can lead and encourage children to learn about inner peace among the hectic, stressful moments in daily life.

One day, my nine-year-old daughter woke up late for her violin practice at school, because she was tired and recovering from the flu, and therefore, I let her sleep in until she was ready to wake. Upon awakening, she realised that she was running late, and started to stress. I looked at her and said: "Sweetie, you're not feeling 100 per cent. If you were, you would have woken up early as usual. So accept that today you will be late, because your body needed the extra sleep. Just know that if you were well, you would not have been late." As soon as she had *accepted* that she couldn't help being late, she immediately let go of the need to worry about being on time and could release the feeling of being stressed out. With this perspective, she was able to resume her calmness and be at peace again. Children can learn how to let go of worry if we guide them.

In general, we need to just embrace our moments in life by being in the present moment, rather than worrying about what will happen next; simply by doing this, we can free up our mind space immediately to resume our clam state and feel peace.

This is what the spiritual leaders refer to when they discuss 'surrendering'. By 'surrendering' yourself to that moment, you can free yourself from the feeling of fighting between being pushed and pulled all at the same time. *It is almost like we live in an illusionary battle within ourselves, when we feel such conflicting emotions that it creates a push and pull feeling inside of our minds, which causes the disruption to our peacefulness.*

Looking at my daughter's example above; in her mind, she was pushing herself to get to school on time and yet at the same time, her tired body was pulling her back to stay in bed longer. But by surrendering to that illusionary battle of push and pull, and by accepting that she had traded punctuality for wellness, and in accepting her new reality of not being able to make it to violin practice on time, she was then able to let go of the feeling of being pushed and pulled and immediately regained her inner peace.

This is not necessary the detail of explanation children need but is a simple example for us as adults to be mindful of, so that can free ourselves of the frustrations of the struggle and conflicting feeling of being pushed and pulled at the same time, and so that we can guide and help our children better in similar situations.

Surrendering to the battle or fight within ourselves, and reaching acceptance are almost like the harmonising 'agents' necessary for happiness, for us to regain inner peace in order to experience joy again.

To give an adult example, if an individual suffers from an unforeseen accident and must face new challenges, it is almost impossible for them to have happiness again unless they can accept their new situation - their 'new reality'. With acceptance, he or she can then work with their current reality to regain their inner peace in order to access happiness again.

It is only when we have a worry-free mind that we can be more relaxed and be in the present moment to connect with ourselves, with others, and with nature and the universe.

"A Hero Does Not Cry, But is Not Afraid to Cry!"

Linda Tomai Duong

"Self-connection is what cultivates the path to self-fulfillment and self-love."

Linda Tomai Duong

"Self-love is infinite love. We must have self-love before we can love others."

Linda Tomai Duong

"We need to turn inwards and tune into OURSELVES in order to access our strength and happiness."

Linda Tomai Duong

"If you cannot be any other kind of expert, be an expert on yourself!"

Linda Tomai Duong

"Happiness is not about looking at what we don't have and wishing we had it, but about appreciating what we already have and finding the strength and resilience to increase the joy we could experience at any given time."

Linda Tomai Duong

"Happiness is already inside you.

Avoid distractions so that you can tune in and access happiness."

Linda Tomai Duong

Chapter 5

Happiness in Connection with Others, with Nature and the Universe

"Be your true-self and you will have better relationships with your spouse, partner, family and friends."

— Linda Tomai Duong

We Need to Smile to be Happy

"When in doubt, just smile."

— Linda Tomai Duong

The simplest way we can connect with each other is to smile. A smile also lifts a person's mood and mind state. It is a very simple thing to do, but we don't do it often enough.

One afternoon, I was feeling particularly tired after driving across from the north side of Sydney to the east side in busy traffic, and spent the day on my feet for six hours before I drive in the peak of the traffic again to get back to the north side to get home. I needed a coffee in order to pick up my energy for the drive. As I approached the café counter, the lady greeted me with the most welcoming and warm smile and it really lifted me up. I felt as if the tiredness that I was lugging around all day was literally lifted off me. I appreciated her smile so much that I actually thanked her for greeting me with the heart-warm smile.

Whenever we see our friends or any other person, whether we know them personally or not, we should just smile. Really, just try it and you will see how simple it is to lift someone's mood. It is just such a simple thing and we all know of the goodness it brings with the positive chain of actions that follows. So simple, yet it has such a powerful and positive carry on effect — but why don't we do it more often? If we want happiness, we need to smile often. Simple.

I have discovered, one of the reasons why we don't smile often enough is because we are almost always too busy with our phones to notice the next person that is coming our way or we are too preoccupied with our own thoughts. "I need to do this and that, and I need to get through this traffic to get to the next appointment," and so on. To be able to do this simple act of smiling, we need to simply slow down our thoughts by taking conscious breaths.

Breathing is natural. We do it without thinking. However, the conscious breath I am referring to is when we deliberately take a pause and breathe intentionally. Yes, I know what you're thinking. "There's so much going on, how can I pause?"

"Amazing things happens when you take a conscious breath. Suddenly, you will feel lighter in your body and you gain more energy to go on."

— Linda Tomai Duong

Taking a conscious breath can lift the weight we feel and break the chain of thoughts that keeps our minds overloaded and flitting from one thought to another; our overcrowded mind is what prevents us from smiling. I normally am a cheerful person but at times I feel as if I have forgotten to smile, and then I realise, it is because my mind is preoccupied with thoughts.

It is good to add this habit of taking a conscious breath each time we are about get into a car, begin a task, or while waiting for the bus and train. In our daily chaotic life, often we just need a moment to still our mind a little… just a moment of quietness to catch our breath or be calm and collected before we move on to another task or project. This way, our minds can gain clarity and we can refocus and function more effectively afterwards, so by pausing just one second, literally, to take a conscious breath we will achieve better results, especially during those overwhelming moments.

Mindful breathing is a proven technique that slows down our thoughts, helping us to stay calm, be collected and gain clarity. That is the magic that happens when we actually pause to take a conscious breath. It is especially beneficial at work when we are moving from one task to another. A conscious breath allows us to have a breather, park a concern or worry aside momentarily, to recollect our thoughts and refocus so that we can continue our day with new, recharged, and uplifted energy, and bring us back to the task at hand with a clearer mind. This helps us to clear our minds frequently as well as we are more aware and are able to 'park' the cluttering thoughts aside.

The conscious breath helps to move more oxygen to the brain, and it also helps improve our concentration and focus. With this practice, we can truly smile as we lighten our weight on the mind and can experience the happy moments in our daily lives when our minds are free from busy and over-crowded thoughts.

There is a saying that we use a lot more muscles to frown than to smile. Whether or not this statement is true, it serves the purpose in encouraging a smile. It definitely *feels* a lot lighter when we smile and heavier when we frown.

Have you ever noticed when you're having a bad day, holding grumpy thoughts, and your body language shows as you connect with others with an annoyed face?

You don't intend it, yet the other party had picked up on your body language and your bad mood. This in turn causes the undesired reaction where they reacted negatively back towards you, because they think your bad mood and negative energy is targeted at them. Not only that, the cycle of negativity begins and is circulated unconsciously when they passed on that grumpiness to someone else or back at you and this can happen without them even thinking about it too. It is instinctive and a natural reflex, and is a totally unconscious action.

However, taking a conscious breathe to smile, we are more calm and collected to be in the present moment, we are more aware of our thoughts, emotions and even aware of our facial expressions that we are making, and can respond consciously rather than by reacting without thinking. When we take a conscious breath and smile, we only pass on positive energy rather than negative ones. Therefore, smiling is one of the simplest ways to connect with others and to achieve calmness.

Smile Brings Friendships and Happiness

"From stranger to friend, we are connected by a smile"

— Linda Tomai Duong

Most friendships start with a smile. When you smile, the other person naturally smiles back. It is the magic of a smile that can turn strangers into friends. You can really brighten up someone's day with a sincere smile. Your heart warms up when you sense the pure joy that your simple, sincere, smile can brighten up someone else's day or even just for a moment of their life – like how the café waitress did for me.

Imagine you bring that heartfelt, sincere, and caring smile to your friend every single time you see each other. Your friend will not only forget about his or her bad moments but will also be cheered up by you and the positive energy that your smile brings. Suddenly, you are both into a conversation before you even know it. You are both engrossed in whatever topic you wish to talk about, discussing and engaging with each other, being together in the present moment. It doesn't matter what the topic is all about. It's about talking, communicating, and sharing with each other wholeheartedly that matters, and being totally present with each other. That is quality time with friends and being in the present moment with each other, truly engaged with each other; this is *connection* on a sincere level. Your friendships will develop at a deeper level, and the quality of your friendships will be much more important than the quantity of friends.

Once the deep connection is developed among friends, you don't need to speak with each other often, but when you do connect, it is like no time has passed between you and your friend. This sincere connection is what leads to true happiness between friends, the authenticity and sincerity with each other. When you have such true feelings with your friends and you know what makes each other happy, that is happiness in friendship and all begins with a smile.

Smiling is also the best winning strategy for social events, at business meetings, and at networking events. It's about turning up with a sincere smile and a positive attitude, being fully present, engaging in conversations, and being joyful as we connect with others. By being the first to show enthusiasm with a sincere smile, we can lift other attendants' moods and pass on the positive effects with the positive energy, resulting in everyone feeling more enthusiastic than they would be, if they were all to keep to themselves.

When we work on promoting positive energy in the room, we effectively co-create a collective of positive energy that promotes more happiness and well-being for each other — and we will most likely form good working relationships with each other as well.

The act of smiling is definitely the simplest way to connect with others and is one of the key elements to developing successful and happy relationships.

Connection with Others

As humans, we crave connections. We are social beings and have been operating this way for as long as history can be traced back. We used to live in tribes and every one played a part as they are contributed to each other. When we connect, there is an *exchange of emotions and energy*. It makes us feel more alive, and relationships form. We crave relationships because they make us feel wanted and important.

We desire relationships greatly because it is a necessity for humans. Connecting with others is where we learn and build our social skills since the early stages of life. Relationships can help us increase our level of confidence and self-esteem when we are valued as a member of the circle of friends. It makes us feel important, worthy and 'good enough' because we are included. Self-esteem and confidence is what we need to be happy, and these are the feelings we get when we connect with others authentically. These same feelings are what motivate us to meet people and connect with others in business networking events.

Connection with Nature and the Universe

"When you're alone, speak to nature

The bird will sing to you and the tree will talk to you

When you're lonely, be at Manly

Be at the beach

Let the beautiful sunset by the beach keep you company

It has magical powers to soothe your heart and soul."

— Linda Tomai Duong

If you like being at the beach like me (my favourite is Manly beach), and you look out to the ocean, and all you can hear is the ocean waves, feel the breeze on your skin, smell the sea salt — and not just hearing the sounds from everybody else at the beach — that's when you are connecting to your environment and being in the present moment. Just you and the ocean, just you and the sound of the waves, or while in a park or garden, there's just you and the flowers or plants. If you're in the wilderness, there's just you and the mountain, or just you and the lake.

When you are comfortable at connecting with yourself, with others and with the environment around you, you can even talk to a tree and feel connected to it. This level of connection can help you find solutions to your challenges in solitude. In fact, this is often when you can be guided to finding your true-self, your higher-self, to hear your own most insightful and intuitive voice that leads you to find answers that may not otherwise be accessible when you are busy-minded and are not present and focused. As have shared in the section – Tune Out to Tune in, on page 75.

Even if you're with someone else, you can still make these connections with your surroundings, in such short time as a few seconds or minutes. The more you do this, the more you experience the beauty of life, and can experience more inner joy and inner peace as go about your daily life. You will also acquire a new habit of clearing your mind regularly and leading yourself to a more positive state of mind frequently. This is when you know that the sound of the ocean soothes your heart and soul. Yet others may not see it or feel the same effect, and it doesn't matter because they don't need to see it or even agree with it. That's your magic moment and your inner peace.

Often a walk in the park, whether it is a short one or a nice long bush walk, is all it takes to connect to nature, or the thought in appreciating the sunshine and the beauty in the flowers. That is enough for us to feel refreshed if you truly appreciate it. Nature gives us a very warm and soothing feeling that brings about inner joy and inner peace, but others may see no big deal about it and, in fact, they may even consider it a boring and lonely time when they don't feel connected with themselves and their surroundings or their nature - the environment.

Knowing that you can simply appreciate nature and your surrounding is enough to give you the connection you need to cast away any feelings of loneliness, it will also help to increase your inner joy that no one can see or take away. It is what *you* appreciate that brings you contentment, and from that, it brings about inner peace. Your inner peace in return is what gives you that inner joy that no one can see or feel except you, and only you. This is a great positive cycle of emotions that promote inner joy and inner peace, and precisely why it is so beneficial to connect with nature and your surroundings.

Even when life throws challenges at us, the external circumstances cannot affect the peace that we hold inside. We can be anywhere, and imagine that natural scenery and immediately we can access our inner peace and inner joy, once we feel connected to nature. We can access our connection wherever we are. *It is what we hold inside our mind that is powerful.*

People often say to me, "Life isn't that simple." I agree, we can't just say: "Let's free up our minds and be connected and we will achieve the ultimate happiness." How about the responsibilities of paying rent, getting a job, feeling secure and belonging, and being recognised that we are important in some way, as well as being valued because we have contributed to others, to feel important one way or another by the end of our lives?

That is why I believe in order for us to continue accessing and activating our true contentment and achieving ultimate happiness, we need to have the support around us. I believe that there are five foundational elements that support us in reaffirming our connections, and allow us to cultivate, and nurture our *currency to happiness*. We can turn to these elements at any time, in order for us to feel love, connection, secure and belonging; so that we can keep accessing or retaining our ultimate happiness, and the good things is we do not need to look far as these five elements are readily for us to access and create any time we want, and they are the five Fs: Family, Friends, Finance, Fitness and Fidelity. Follow me through the following chapters to discover these foundations to grow your currency to achieve even more happiness.

TIPS:

Be outdoors as much as possible.

Enjoy your own company so that you can enjoy connecting.

Lean on nature to tune out in order to tune in.

"If you want to be happy

Smile!

It's Free!"

"Connecting with nature is the quickest way that leads us to achieve inner peace."

Linda Tomai Duong

Chapter 6

Happiness in FAMILY Connection

"Family is what we fight for. We will do anything for our family."

— *Linda Tomai Duong*

Family Connection

First of the five elements that supports us in being able to have self-love and self-connection is *Family*. Family is what gives us support and a safe place to return to. A place where we begin to build our identity, confidence, and to form strong bonds and connections with parents, care givers and close relatives. It is a place where we learn about self-love as a child and about loving others, and developing emotional awareness skills, as we receive the support to learn about resilience.

When asked, any parent will tell you, it is his or their family that they strive for. Their family is what gets them up every morning, going back to the same job every day, whether they like the job or not.

Different Types of Family

Family structure is much more complex these days. However, it does not matter which model you define as a family. There are biological parents, step parents, and same gender parents. There are families with children from adoptions, and there are multi-cultural adoptions as well.

I know many families, including mine, which follow or adopt more than one cultural value. There are also families that live around the world. One family in particular really represents global citizenship. The mother is of Chinese heritage but was born in America, and the father is an American man with Greek heritage. They gave birth to their child in Rio, and then moved to Australia with their young son where they now reside. However, it didn't matter where they lived. What mattered was that they stayed connected with each other, and formed a strong bond with each other and that they consider themselves a family wherever they are on the globe, whether they are all together in one country or separated in two different countries.

It is the connection maintained in each family that keeps their bond strong. In contrast, lack of connections is what causes families to fall apart. Some people can be living in the same house but don't feel connected with each other at all.

Connection with Non-Biological Family

Most of us grow up with our biological family, while others may not. Did you know that you can actually *re-create* your own ideal family? I don't mean getting married and starting your own family unit. Of course, that is the 'happy ever after' kind of family connection. However, what I am referring to is for those people who have lost their parents through unfortunate and unforeseen circumstances, or for those who have parents but feel they missed out on that special bond and connection. *You can re-create that bond and connection if you wish*, whether it is with your own parents if there is a second chance, or with siblings and relatives such as grandparents or aunts and uncles. Or even with others that are not biologically related.

A family connection can be created by establishing strong connections with people that you feel you are able to have special bonds with.

Just like my mum did. Growing up in Vietnam, my mum lost her mother at the young age of eight. Her father was the farmers' landlord, which meant that he was quite wealthy for their time in that little village. With such status, it was common for men to have more than one wife. Due to this shame, my maternal grandmother fell into depression, and sadness was what eventually took her life. It is one of the worst tragedies in life to lose her mother at such a young age.

Feeling incredibly lost, all my mum could do was cry, cry and cry every night. The saddest thing was that she had to hide her grief at losing her mum. She was afraid to cry during the day in case the mistress would get upset or angry at her. She saved it all up for night time in bed. She used to tell us that every morning she had to bring her pillow out to dry in the sun because it would have been soaking wet from her tears throughout the night.

Losing your mum at any age can cause anyone to feel sad, become resentful and angry and not able to open up to others, let alone the fact that she was only eight years old. Surprisingly, as sad and sorrowful as she was, she still opened up eventually and connect with the people around her. Mostly to the one and only family member that she had a strong bond and felt connected to. It was an older *sister*. This sister was not a biological sister at all; she was the maid of the household that soon became my mother's sister.

During my parents' time, in the early 1920s, it was common that the poor parents actually *gave* their children away to the wealthy families, as the poor parents had no means of caring for the *extra child* when there were already other children and elderly family members to look after.

Ultimately, it was seen as a chance for the new addition of the family to have a better chance in life. So the wealthy families *helped out* by taking these children in when the child was a little older. And in return, they offered financial assistance to the child's family to help improve their situation. The child who was sent off to the wealthy family would grow up to become a maid or a helper in the household and, in many cases, they would lose touch with their biological family. In other cases, when the two families didn't live too far from each other, the maid or helper may go back and visit his or her own family with permission from their adopted family.

This sister came as a maid but became the older sister who looked after my mum. They both were lucky and unlucky all at the same time. The older sister was lucky because she was never treated as a maid, but also unlucky because there was no female adult figure to guide her in her life. Not only that, she then had to look after a child a few years younger than her. It was the same for my mum. She very unlucky to have lost her own mother but lucky that she suddenly had a sister to look after her.

The two girls bonded and grew to have the utmost respect for each other. Even in theirs 60's, their love, concern, and respect for each other was deeper than any biological sisters I have ever witnessed. If only all family members could connect with such a deep level of love and care, sincerity and authenticity, and respect for each other, we would have very happy families with the ultimate connection and happiness in family.

It was said that my mum was the richest girl in that village, because of her father's status. But, she was also the most unfortunate and saddest girl to have lost her mum at such young age.

Luckily, with the love of this *sister*, she wasn't the saddest girl after all. With the love and care she received, she became happier each day. And even though with such tragedy happened to her so early in life, she still grew up to become an amazing individual, mother, grand-mother, and great-grand-mother.

I often wondered about how she was able to grow into such a warm, loving and cheerful person and ultimately an amazing mum of 10 children of her own. She was a very open and warm, caring and intuitive mum. Together with my dad, they raised 10 children in a resource limited country, and yet all of their children were well-educated and well cared for. She was just an incredible woman and parent; no words can articulate my gratitude for her. Sadly, she passed away in 2004 in Vietnam, in her birth hometown and in her bed sleeping peacefully, at the age of 75.

Meanwhile, as I am writing this book to share with you, my amazing dad is residing at a nursing home in Sydney, celebrating his 97th birthday this year.

The reason why I share this story with you is not only to celebrate a great life but also in the hope that *it will inspire more love, more connections and more trust,* because there are many people who suffer in silence and eventually become affected by depression. Connecting with others offers healing. By simply sharing life stories with each other, we let each other know that – "I am going through the same thing, and that I am not the only one." And that there is always someone there for us to share and connect with. It reminds us that we are here to support one another, and not to live in isolation.

I am also hoping that by sharing her story here, *it can inspire more hope, and more faith, and more kindness to be seen.* There are many others have also experienced separation and loss from their own biological family due to a variety of life events such as terrorism or civil war, natural disasters, et cetera. I sincerely hope that this story will inspire you to reach out and connect with others in a way that will serve you and so that you can serve them too, with the intention of bringing happiness to all who need it.

If we strive to live in a world of love and connection with each other, the world will be a much better place. There will be less isolation and less depression. It will be a place where we all feel loving and connected with each other. Perhaps I am a dreamer, but wouldn't that be a beautiful place? A place where love resides with everyone feeling that we are connected with one another.

Just as John Lennon sings: "*You may say that I'm a dreamer, but I'm not the only one. I hope someday you'll join us, and the world will live as one*". You and I can dream of the same dream too, that someday, we will all be connected as one.

In the 1980s, many refugees from Asia were adopted by their new families as they arrived into Australia. Some of my Vietnamese friends also found new families in Canada and America as well. We don't often think of it, but yes, we can absolutely re-create the ideal family that we want and create the connections we need and yearn for.

These days, more and more exchange students study overseas, where they will stay and live with their host family. This is the opportunity to create and connect with the family environment you desire if you stay abroad and miss your own family, even just for the short while is still worthwhile — to feel love, to share, to give and receive love is always worthwhile of the effort. You can take the relationship as far as you wish if you stay open and connect on a deeper level with your host family or your guest-child, so that you both can have more joy and more happiness in the process.

"The more family connections we create, the more bonds we build towards, The Currency to Happiness."

— *Linda Tomai Duong*

If you are from foster families, these are your chances in re-creating the ideal family that you wished for, and it all begins with sincere, authentic connections. Sometimes, all it takes is to reach out with a sincere smile or a warm hug to begin this wonderful connection journey with your foster family.

Following is another heart-warming story I would like to share.

Phoebe* (not her real name) grew up a very traditional, and closed-minded family. When she was born, her father could not look at her for the first 10 days of her life, and she had to go and live with her aunt for this period. This is most the fragile, and vulnerable time for babies. A time when babies need their mothers most. Yet, she could not come home as her parents couldn't face the new reality of their lives. Her father was so devastated because her parents by now had gave birth to three girls.

When I first heard this story, I was very surprised, as I thought this would have been a common story in the past, in China or Asian countries, but I did not expect to learn that this happens in Western countries such as Australia, too. This shows that as human, we all have common emotions regardless which country we are born or live in.

Phoebe's parents were wealthy and had supported her schooling but, emotionally, her father disowned her. The pair eventually separated, and her mother moved on with a new man. Phoebe's sister was eight years older than her and she was the one that had raised Phoebe. This is such a coincidental similarity to my mum's story.

Phoebe went to boarding school when she was about 10 years old. It was known as the "country's strictest boarding school" ran by nuns, and she stayed there for five years. During this period, she prayed fervently and her earliest memories are of talking with God, and she had wanted to be a nun herself.

As if destined to happen, when her sister got married and Phoebe's new brother-in-law didn't want Phoebe to live with them, so eventually, with some twists and turns, Phoebe ended up as an exchange student and went to Denmark when she was 15 years old.

There, she had the chance to meet this incredibly kind-hearted man just after her 16th birthday. He took her into his home and shared his family with Phoebe. One thing that he insisted on was that Phoebe was to speak Danish, something Phoebe said she is eternally grateful for.

He tried to help Phoebe to gain her Danish citizenship back then, but it was not approved and in the end, she was given 14 days to leave Denmark in her early twenties, which she described as one of the saddest days of her life. Since then, she has been back to Denmark 10 times and has lived there twice. She had always wanted to go back and see her beautiful Danish family.

When Phoebe got married, her foster father came with his family and friends from Copenhagen to Sydney to give her away. He had shown her how to be a nice person. He had also taught her about how to love without limits and how to laugh and live with abundance.

Sadly, on February 22nd 2003, Phoebe's 'adopted father' passed away. Phoebe got to his funeral within 32 hours. She flew from Sydney to Copenhagen. While transiting in Tokyo, she begged the stewardess to let her board another plane as her plane was not due to depart until the next day, except business class passengers were allowed to catch alternative flights to England. Phoebe was desperate to see her adopted father once more, even though she knew, she could no longer talk to him and she could no longer hear his voice as he had departed this earth-life. Luckily, in England, she was put her on a flight in a business class to Copenhagen as they could see the tragedy and the need for her to race there.

*Name has been changed to protect her privacy.

These two stories make me think of all the individuals from the orphanage, or those who are born to emotionally and physically abusive parents, and those that had emotionally-disturbed parents and any other individuals who need to hear this story to bring back hope, faith and trust in life. These two stories are especially for you.

The two stories above, really reminds us that if we stay open and are willing to connect, *we can really re-create and change our 'pre-determined' destiny.*

I too was fortunate, to have experienced this extended parental love apart from those of my parents'. Since my teenage years, I was often showered with love from either my friends' mothers or my much older friends, and even from the mothers of the in-laws of my siblings; with comments such as; "You could be my daughter!" or "I wish you were my daughter." And "I know I already have a daughter, but I wouldn't mind to have another one because we talk to each other so well!" and more…. It is wonderful to be able to connect personally and deeply with each other whether we are biologically related or not, as it adds so much more joy and meaning to life.

"Connection brings happiness."

— Linda Tomai Duong

Connection with Biological Family

We need to make an effort to stay connected. We take for granted that as families we naturally are connected. Yes, as siblings and children to our parents, we are all biologically connected to each other — but is every one really connecting with each other? Does each person in the family really know what's going on with the other family members? Most often, everyone is too busy with their own lives to know what is happening with another family member's life, especially when it comes to adult children.

One simple family routine that my mum introduced to our family is very helpful for staying connected with each other, and it is family meal time. Meal time is connection time for our family and I know it is for many families in many different cultures too. However, due to the busyness of the modern life, we tend to eat on the go and therefore, quality family meal time has been compromised. So this following story is to remind us all to reintroduce the value of family meal time.

After we settled into our new life in Sydney, my mum requested that we must communicate to her on a daily basis and said: "This is a new country to me and I don't speak the language. I can't learn it as fast as you do. So, each day you must come home and tell me what you did at work or at school. What kind of news you heard for the day. You need to share with me so that I can keep up-to-date too, and can follow the world as well as your progress." Every day, dinner time was when we all took turns to tell her and each other our updates. It was nothing formal, just casual conversations and sharing about our day. But her request made us feel more aware of each other's updates, and encouraged us to share with her and with the family more. It was a very easy and effortless way to stay connected in the family.

Apart from having an excuse to talk, to reflect on the day, and to share about the recent events, our chats easily led to discussions of other topics, some serious, some not so serious. We touched on politics if it's voting time. Mostly, it brought up old memories; we compared the differences with life in Australia and life in Vietnam, and it gave us a chance to share and it became quite therapeutic for our hearts too. Especially when we a bad day or a challenging issue to face with.

These days, of course, it would be harder for my siblings and me to do daily dinner catch ups as we are now all married, have our own children, and live in different cities. Nevertheless, this is the routine I apply to my own family now, and it has really reminded us to stay open and keeping connecting with each other on a daily basis, either at meal times or during our weekly family game time.

We also do some formal family talks once a while, where we sit in a circle and take turns to simply update each other. The purpose is to address any issues we have with each other, or to share a thought, a wish, or an idea. These meetings are run more like an office meeting, where the children take turn to chair the meeting. They also make sure no one is talking over another person, and only one person is allowed to talk at a time. It is nice to see the children introduced and initiated these meetings at the ages of six and eight years old. They were keen to keep hosting these meetings because it made them feel equally important as the adults, especially when they get to chair the meeting and remind someone else that they need to wait for their turn to talk.

We also have boy's days/nights out, and girl's days/nights out, where my husband and son will do their own activity and I spend time with my daughter. Other times we have FDT (father-daughter time) and MST (mum-son time). We also have times when the children play with each other without the distraction of technology. These are a few simple reminders of family rituals that can help family members to stay open with their communications and connecting with each other on a regular basis.

It all comes back to connection. Connection is what help us to open up and enables us to stay close to the people we love, whether they are biologically related to us or not. Connecting with people who care for us and us for them make us feel happier and feel more fulfilled.

Happiness in the Family — Acceptance of Ourselves and Others

One big factor that helps with good family connection is acceptance. Acceptance means living with, and valuing the differences in ourselves and in others. Acceptance can sometimes make or break relationships, particularly with life partners. Same goes with family and friends and even with children. However, the most important acceptance of all is *self-acceptance.*

Happiness in the Family — Self-Acceptance

As a child, it is natural that we need our parents' acceptance because with acceptance, it tells us that we are loved unconditionally, which makes us feel secure, giving us a sense of positive self-esteem and positive self-worth.

The two most direct ways that we interpret acceptance as a child, are shown in the forms of praise and approval. When we are children, our parents teach and demonstrate to us what is okay and what is not okay; we are dependent on them to guide us and help us navigate the world around us.

Our parents' approval communicates to us what kind of behaviours were acceptable and pointed out those that were unacceptable, and this process kept us safe and protected us from getting into trouble as we learnt not to violate other's comfort and the laws around us.

Other times, our parents gave us praise when we have done the right thing, which confirmed to us that we have done well and that left us with some proud moments. These responses from our parents are essential for our development during the early years of life.

However, as adults, we are no longer dependent on our parents' approval and praise to function. We now can actually choose to *detach from the need for acceptance* from our parents and focus instead on our own self-acceptance.

Looking at this from a logical and practical sense, basically self-acceptance is embracing who we are, our strengths as well as our imperfections, which means we need to be kind to ourselves and allow ourselves the time and patience for our life journey; which is a work-in-progress and still to be carried out.

As we know, in order to achieve happiness, we need to feel our own inner peace, but we cannot be at peace if we do not accept who we are. This does not mean "take me as I am or leave me alone". Nor do we use it as an excuse to stop nurturing our mind and body, which in effect ignoring our own personal growth. It simply means, stop seeking acceptance and approval from our parents, for two reasons:

We are no longer a child. We now can make decisions or learn to make decisions on our own and can take responsibility for ourselves.

Our life is still evolving, which means, it is a work-in-progress and still to be carried out. Therefore, there is no need for the 'overall' appraisal and praise, and we can take away the weight of acceptance as to whether we are doing 'good enough' or not.

Every case and everyone is different. However, one of the reasons why we still seek parental acceptance in adulthood is because we are still attached to our mind's inner child. We are attached to our childhood memories, and for whatever reason, or whatever happened in the past, we didn't receive the acceptance that we looked for, and without realising it, that need for parental acceptance has lingered on, into adulthood and has stayed with us.

Realising this now, it is the time to release that attachment of a child's need to parental acceptance once and for all. Please take note that, releasing the need for our parents' approval does not mean we are detaching or dis-owning our parents. It simply means to grow into our independent-self, so that you can feel free to move on as an adult with confidence, and to be able to do what you truly wish to do, and be free, to be the person you are meant to be.

Rather than continually seeking parental acceptance, it is better to use that time and energy to work on personal development and growth, and tune in regularly, to check in, and see whether we are staying on course or not, and making sure that we are keeping in line of our values with what we do, as we serve our purpose in life, whatever that may be.

We can help our parents to accept the "new" version of us by staying connected to them, and keeping them updated on what we do and staying connected through ways of communication and sharing updates in our lives. We all have the need to love and be loved. It is a healthy balance between loving and being loved, along with developmental growth that can transform ourselves in effective ways.

TIPS:

Finding Peace in Conflicts between Parent and Child — Gaining Solace

"Most illness is just stress from not living in harmony."

— Bruce H. Lipton

In a family where there is more than one child, it is almost certain that every child will have a slightly different view of their parents. The same goes for the parents. They will say that they love all of their children in the same way, yet, if you ask them about their relationship with each child, you will inevitably hear that the relationship with each child is different. This is because each individual has a different set of personality traits, even if they're twins. Each child's personality and behaviours evoke different responses from the parents, and that creates a different chain of reactions. This is one of the factors that contribute to sibling rivalry, which we will discuss later.

For Parents – Releasing the Guilt with Reflective Parenting Thoughts

Many parents I spoke to are still holding on the guilt. As parents, if we have done all we could, given the situation that we were in, then we need to accept that any unintended mistakes that happened were due to situational circumstances. Acknowledge them, forgive yourself, and grow from those reflections so that you can move on. Feeling guilty or staying in a guilty mode does not serve any purpose, nor does it give any long term benefits. Reflecting on what has worked and what hasn't gives us insights into our situation that no others could. Throughout the growing years, I remember, especially at *siesta* times in Vietnam, my mum would often share with us her thoughts on things that worked and on things that didn't work.

During that time when my parents ran the corner shop that offered wholesale supplies to street vendors as well as selling to individuals in the neighbourhood, you have to be on high alert at all times. There were the corrupted officials who tried to create opportunities to have you pay them for apparently the 'wrong things' you did in your business, which you were not aware of yourself, or the tricky traders that looked for opportunities to make some extra gains, as well as the small cheaters that may take the opportunity to take whatever they can.

My mum's daily reflections taught us more lessons than we can learn in school or anywhere else. Through sharing her thoughts on why a certain business trading was a silly move or why certain things work better this way than that way. She had demonstrated to us how to think reflectively and how we can do our best, should the same incidents occur again.

Looking back, her open communication was like none that I have known of in those times. Back then, most adults don't include children in their talks, let alone sharing business operations or decision-making thought processes with them.

Born in the late 1920s, my mum was an amazingly open-minded and inclusive individual (of all ages and genders) — she was far advance of her time in terms of being inclusive. Although there were 10 children, and the eldest was 20 years older than the youngest, and I am the second youngest in the family. Never did I feel too small to listen and to learn decision-making skills in business. Neither did I ever feel I was too little to help out. This background learning made me an entrepreneur at the age of eight, which I will share in another book.

My mum had also shared her emotions of her happy and unhappy times in an open, authentic and appropriate manner, and not just loading it on us. She also reminded us that no matter what unforeseen or unfortunate circumstances happened to us, we do not wish it upon others. It was her reflective thinking style of sharing that has empowered me to become a more intuitive and insightful individual and parent that I am today.

My reflective habits have enabled me to handle my daily challenges with a habitual thought process in asking myself: "OK, what works and how come that didn't?" or "I want things to go this way but s/he wants it the other way, what happened there?" "What purpose did that serve?" And "whose benefits was it for?"

Whether the outcome is a successful one or not, this is the thought process that I have followed while growing up. I've carried it out in my adult life and into my businesses as well.

This basic reflective parenting style can really help us re-examine what had happened and how or why we did what we did as parents. Once you have recognized the reasons for the 'flaw' or mistake that has happened. There are two things we can do:

Acknowledge the mistake and apologies to the children involved.

Acknowledge what had happened, grow from that and forgive yourself.

I have seen parents that live with guilt and there really is no value in doing that. I would be much better to use the time and energy to make up for the relationship.

Using the reflective parenting tips now can allow us to gain insight into parenting our children better so that we can be more in tune with them from here on.

For (Adult) Children — Be Free

It is amazing how many adults are still yearning for parents' love, approval, and praise. Whatever happened has happened. It is in the past. Recognising that for whatever reason it was, that your parent(s) may have said or did things to hurt you, know and accept that most parents don't intend to hurt their child if they have a healthy mind. Things happen in life. Most likely, their actions were limited to a variety of contributing factors such as; their old customs/beliefs, bias or wrong views and advice from others, limited knowledge, and/or financial stress et cetera. This is not to give them excuses for their wrongdoing but for you to find a way to elicit some kind of empathy, to comfort your heart, and mainly for closure to your wound. So that you can move on. Feeling upset or angry, and staying in a resentful mode does not add benefits.

Whatever happened that made you feel unhappy, it is time to let go of all those old feelings, hurtful emotions and unhappy old memories.

Imagine you bag up all of those unhappy emotions and unhappy memories and take the bag out on a boat and send it out to sea. Let it drift, drift, drift away. So far, far away that you will NEVER, EVER, EVER see it again.

While at sea, a strong wind blows the bag open, and all those old emotions and old memories flew away, all dissipated into thin air. Leaving you all clear of heaviness in your body. Now you feel light and free and renewed.

This is your new beginning to a happier self.

As a child, if you have suffered from some bad treatments before, then you have held on to those memories long enough. *It is time to let those feelings go.*

Reset, Take action, Begin again.

"Cut the cord, drop the rock and move on."

— Linda Tomai Duong

For (Adult) Siblings – No More Sibling Rivalry

Sibling rivalry begins in childhood but it doesn't end there. It gets carried on into adulthood and continues on. Let's just call it for quite here, shall we? No more comparing and competing with each other. When we were little children, we couldn't help but compare who gets more of what, and who is better at this and that or who is smarter or prettier. The list can go on. Of course, not everyone has this problem but if you do, it is time to detach and let this old childhood fights go. As adults now, you don't need to hold on to these non-serving memories any more.

Sibling rivalry in young children is almost unavoidable, unless you are the only child in the family. Every case is unique as it depends on the parents' different circumstances. For example, when a first child is born, the parents' financial situation was good, and so they were more relaxed and able to give the child more time, more attention and more affection. However, by the time the second child comes into the family, the parents' time, energy and money were all divided, and so, naturally, the second child doesn't receive as much time, attention and affection as the first child did. By the time the third child comes along, the scale of things increases or decreases, depends on which way you look at things. This is only a very quick example to illustrate the point.

It could also be the opposite situation, such as the parents weren't as experienced and knowledgeable in looking after the first new baby, and so he or she didn't get the same level of thorough care as the younger siblings did.

It is only natural that the eldest gets more of whatever - be it on the positive side or the negative side of things. Therefore, there is no point in comparing and competing with each other. But as little children, we had no knowledge of this and it was a natural thing to do, to compare just about everything.

The eldest child may be more spoiled for being the first precious child, but also gets more responsibilities as they grow older, whereas the youngest one gets more attention from the older siblings because she's the baby of them all, and as we compare, let's not forget about the middle ones. How about the middle ones? What happens to the middle ones then, especially when there are 10 children? The middle ones don't need to take on as much responsibility because the older ones take care of them. They also don't get as much attention because it goes to the last baby. So they seem to be the ones that get neglected. They become the quiet and not so noticeable ones.

Middle children from large Asian families often feel like they are ignored, not important, or worse, 'invisible'. But should they feel that way? For sure, not. Being in the middle, they're the bridge, the harmonising agents, and the mediators. This is especially shown in the western families, middle children become more independent as they observers and 'fend for themselves'. They tend to think outside of the box and feel less pressure to conform, and are more empathetic from observing the older and the younger siblings, allowing them to develop great interpersonal skills as makes them excellent team players. Of course ever case id different but these are my observations.

Back to sibling rivalry, there is no need really. It's like you are trying to work out who is more important? The farmer who grew the crops, the transporter, or the shopkeeper? Each of them will say they're the most important one. Reality is, they each are just as important as the other. We don't get to enjoy fresh food without any of them if we live in the big city where we don't grow our own fresh food. So, you can stop comparing. Each has their own importance with their own unique abilities and characteristics.

With regards to what order you were born in the family and who gets what, it just cannot be helped. So, why not just accept the reality of things and be at peace with it? Let go of this childhood attachment to sibling rivalry. Unless you're from the royal and monarch families, then that will make a big difference, but, even so, you cannot control or change the order that you were born in, so the choices are to accept it and have peace or to resent and to struggle.

Sometimes parents use competitiveness between their young children as a form of encouragement, a 'tactic' to motivate the child who needs to put in more effort and they say things such as: "Look, Ben has got his shoes on already, and we're all ready to go but you. Hurry up!" While this is done with good intentions, it can result in negative side effects and the repetitiveness of this nature is what can contribute to sibling rivalry in the long run.

Below are a few summarised examples on the reasons why sibling rivalry stays on into adulthood:

• Each child feels unequal amounts of attention and love from their parents.

• Each child is competing to define who they are as an individual. As they grow older, they try to find their own talents and status, such as who earns more or who is smarter and who is more successful.

• Family dynamics. For example, one child's arrival may have reminded a parent of a particularly difficult time, even though this was situational and neither was it the parent's fault nor the child's, and yet that may subconsciously influence how the parent treats or relates to that child.

As adults, now we have gain the knowledge and understanding some of the causes for sibling rivalry, we can forgive and forget. At the end of the day, they are someone we call *family* after all, and we all want to live with peace and joy, and not in anger and resentment.

Finding Peace in Conflicts with Other Adult Family Members

As family members, it is one of the most precious relationships that lasts a life time. Not even husband and wife have that kind of guarantee. Yet, sometimes there is this bittersweet relationship happening. Sometimes you get on well with each other. Other times you fight badly with each other. That is just the cycle of human relationships. Of course, there are those relationships that never saw a fight like my mum and her incredibly loving sister. On the opposite end, there are also those that can't see each other eye to eye, even though they are family.

How can we have happiness within the family when you are in those conflicting situations?

There are two choices we can make:

Have a good talk. Communicate openly and truthfully but respectfully with each other to resolve the issue together. Do allow time for the 'heat' to cool down first, before you get together for the talk, and allow patience to have more than one meeting for the issue to be resolved.

If option a) is not an option then move on. Make a choice but **never** stay unhappy.

It may take time but as soon as you can, let go of all the hurt and resentment so that you can feel lighter. Release all the heavy, unhappy energy and let it go because it is draining and tiring.

Reach out to friends, relatives, and people who care and understand you. Reach out to new friends and old ones, mainly ones that you can connect to. This is not to suggest that you load your emotional 'baggage' on another person but instead build new relationships for another beginning, to have happier times, and to inspire renewed energy for vitality.

Sometimes, it is just not possible to forget some events or forget some actions that have happened in the past. Whatever choice you make, the main focus is to have peace within yourself.

Each person has their own point of view and their reasons for doing what they did and each person is always right in their own eyes or has their reasons and excuses for what has occurred.

Whether to forgive or not to forgive, it is a choice. Give yourself this clarity so that you can feel empowered, rather than feeling like a victim, stuck and dis-empowered. Once the decision is made, be okay with it so that you can have peace.

Bearing in mind though, if you choose not to forgive, you will still feel heavy as you're living in the past. So, it's only a matter of time until you must take the path to forgiveness, because whatever happened has happened. Do you keep staying there or do you move on? Time will help us be ready. However, the sooner you can forgive, the sooner you can move towards the lighter heart state and find renewed energy to be happy again.

Imagine yourself old and frail, sitting alone in your home or nursing home, nearing the end of your life. Wouldn't it be nice for you to have your family to come and visit you? And, most importantly, don't you want to leave this earth in peace when your last day on earth comes? Not easy to do, but that's the path to take.

"Forgiveness is what brings peace from within."

– Linda Tomai Duong

"The more family connections we create the more bonds we build towards the currency to happiness."

Linda Tomai Duong

"Let go of the feelings and emotions that no longer serve you.

Open yourself up to receive and embrace happier feelings."

Linda Tomai Duong

"Connection is what keeps our souls alive and provides the answers that we are seeking."

Linda Tomai Duong

"Forgiveness is what brings peace from within."

Linda Tomai Duong

Chapter 7

Happiness in Friendship with Authenticity and Sincerity

"Happiness in friendship is when friends truly understand each other."

— Linda Tomai Duong

Second of the five elements that supports us in being able to have more self-love and create more connections is Friends.

Friendship with Authenticity and Sincerity

"True friendship is when someone knows you better than you know yourself and they have your best interests at heart, whether you are in a crisis or not."

— *Linda Tomai Duong*

Friends are there to support each other. Like they say, 'it takes two to tango' and that 'one-way street' doesn't work as it causes traffic jams, congestion and frustration. Also, having someone to trust and confide in, gives us a sense of faith and loyalty. Friendships take time and effort to build, and to stay connected, especially if we want strong and respectful friendships. Therefore, it is not about quantity but quality, and connecting from a place of authenticity is key.

It is often said that *friendship is like a garden*. It needs watering and nurturing and, given time and patience, the end result is as beautiful as a garden.

Friends can also help shape who we are and that is why parents often say: "*Choose your friends wisely*". At the same time, we need to be the wise friend for others too, if we would like to have a good friend. We also need to be willing to be the friend that we wished for. Always remember that while we choose others, they may be choosing us as well. As the old saying goes: "Treat others as you would like to be treated yourself."

A considered comment goes a long way. The comments we make, and the feelings we pass on to others, whether randomly or intentionally, can have an impact on those around us. When we feel good about something, we would naturally say pleasant things to others, which directly or indirectly makes them feel good, and in turn, they will then pass that uplifting mood on to the next person that they interact with. It is like a chain of reactions; so let's be mindful to keep the chain of reactions a positive one, rather than a negative one.

"Kindness in words creates confidence. Kindness in thinking creates profoundness. Kindness in giving creates love."

— Tao Te Ching

Other times we may also need to be aware of the fine difference between assertiveness and aggressiveness. Assertive people state their viewpoints, while still being respectful to others. Aggressive people ignore others' viewpoints in favour of their own and can be seen to be attacking others. While passive people don't state their viewpoints at all.

When we can connect with others authentically and sincerely, we allow ourselves to express our emotions and feelings truthfully and, hence, others will feel comfortable and encouraged to do the same. Open hearted, genuine and respectful friendships will most likely last longer and can become those strong relationships that we consider as our extended family in times of need. Especially when our immediate family are not available to us, these close friends are there for us as our extended family. This is how we can lead the way in searching for the ultimate happiness in friendships. As we stay connected with each other, we will all become happier with each other.

Expressing Ourselves Authentically, not Showing Anger Randomly

Expressing ourselves authentically is about managing our feelings and emotions to gain peace and happiness. When we are experiencing strong negative emotions such as rage or anger, trying to take a deep breath and counting to 10 to hold off our temper during those moments until we can feel stable can really help us to regain our balance. Letting those undesirable emotions pass or take a pause to have some quiet moments to detach from the negative emotions before we communicate more with the involved party, can also help to prevent those hurtful words that anger evokes.

When we feel anger, it is not an ideal time to talk, as anger generally does not resolve or address the problems. Anger is usually associated with us hiding fear or vulnerability and wanting to exert control.

Below is a quick example of an extract of such a dialogue;

"I don't like what you're saying! It hurts me inside to hear what you say, so I am telling you loudly now that I don't like it! You better stop that or I will get even angrier!

This is the exact behaviour that *disconnect* us from each other, and is the exact opposite to what we want. What we want is to express ourselves truthfully and considerately with respect so that we can understand each in order to stay connected with each other. When these moments occurs, it is best to go outside. By being out side with fresh air, spending time in nature can help us shift our mind towards a more positive mood and lower our stress level. It is one of the most effective and immediate stress-relievers. Once we have calmed down in our private moments, we then can respond more positively to things and we can be honest with ourselves about how we truly feel. That is how we can lead ourselves back to focus on connecting with our inner-selves for self-comfort. When we open up to ourselves and connect with our inner-self, we can experience healing that is different from the help that we receive from others. We will also begin to gain clarity and insights into our deeper emotions and feelings, and we can 'go home' to our *old selves* prior to the eruption of the anger. We then can become more calmed and collected to open up, to reconnect with the involved party. When someone is calm, it is always more pleasant to be with.

As a child, we need others to comfort us when we are hurt or sad, and we demand attention and we want to be acknowledged immediately. As an adult, what we need is to allow ourselves the time and space to express our hurtful feelings or those moments of sadness, and to acknowledge those challenging moments ourselves. This is by far better than to be ignoring the unpleasant emotions, doing other things to keep ourselves busy and to distract ourselves from feeling those emotions, or bury all those feelings. Burying these hurtful, sad, or undesirable feelings does not make us tougher or stronger, yet, it does have the tendency to build up to become more depressive emotions and causes unnecessary carry-on effects.

Once we take some quiet moments to acknowledge how we truly feel, we can articulate and deal with those feelings and emotions in a more calm and controlled manner. Otherwise, the disappointment can lead to irritability, frustration, or acting out and speaking offensively to others unintentionally such as the following example: Mandy is clearly upset that her boyfriend didn't turn up for their date but she pretended that she's 'cool' about it, and yet she let her emotions out on Lara, her housemate when she had returned home. Then, Lara got upset and grumpy that she has been spoken to rudely, but all the while, is worried about Mandy's change of mood, as she has sensed something had happened. She then inadvertently passed that grumpiness and unhappy energy on to her boyfriend. The negative chain of reaction and energy simply got passed on. As you can see, we can easily impact others with how we show our emotions, either positively or negatively. Therefore, it is much better to express it appropriately and get the right help when needed.

What if Mandy was to take a breath and ask her friend Lara, to lend her an ear with appropriate manners, and then shares openly by saying: "*I am disappointed that my boyfriend didn't turn up for our date, and I feel let down and hurt.*" This would have given Lara an opportunity to give her a hug, offer some comforting words and advice. They even may have been able to take the opportunity to build deeper bonds. Mandy's unhappy experience comprises a whole mix of several emotions; hurt, anger, and disappointment, possibly even worry for her date's safety as well.

Not expressing ourselves appropriately can cost us the love and care that we need and deserve, during those painful and vulnerable moments, and at the same time, robs others of the opportunity to show us the love and concern they feel for us.

Being our authentic-selves doesn't mean speaking inconsiderately. It simply means being able to express our feelings without the worry or concern of being judged, which is comforting and allowing us to be who we really are. There are many other ways to express our feelings and emotions, even when we are on our own, including going for a run or a jog, boxing and kick boxing, diving into the pool, surfing at the beach, or going to the park with your dog or go horse-riding. Mainly to be with nature, with animal, and being outside connecting with nature and all beings.

Other times, we can simply express ourselves by listening to music, to either dance the excitement off or soothe our heart and soul in times of need, or get a professional manicure and pedicure to pamper and comfort ourselves. It can even be as simple as stopping for a cup of coffee or tea to acknowledge the feelings and emotions that are surfacing and requiring our attention. Whether we are feeling down low, on top of the world or simply overwhelmed, a pause is all we need to comfort ourselves or have a cup of coffee to acknowledge and celebrate with the thought of; "yay! I did it!" when we have done a good job. The simple act of self-acknowledgement is one of the simplest and most effective ways to stay connected with ourselves.

However, some of us may prefer to talk to a trusted person or professional to help us to go through the process of letting all the heavy emotions out, especially in times of grieving and complicated situations, and to gain further comfort; before we are ready to revisit and deal with the problem again. Whichever way you choose, at the end of the exercise, the goal is to feel better and lighter, refreshed, and ready to reconnect with the world again.

Whether you choose to connect with another person, an animal, or nature, *just be outside to feel the fresh air, and let go of all the negative emotions* - there is sure enough emphasis on this but really you will feel much better than keeping it all inside. It helps us to clear our minds and process the intense emotions that would otherwise block us from moving forward, towards a happier state.

Be Open and Be Understood

When we act 'cool' but in reality we are not, it makes things complicated. Not only are the people who do care for us, unable to extend their care, but it also confuses them because they usually can figure out what is happening.

That is when I hear the suggestion of 'be vulnerable'. I guess what they are trying to say is to be open, let your guards down and drop the walls. Let go of the fear of others seeing your true feelings, so that people who care about you can comprehend what you are facing and understand what exactly is bothering you, so that they can be more informed and can offer help more appropriately. Hence the suggestion of *be vulnerable.*

Although with good intentions, we still need to be mindful of how we use this phrase — be vulnerable. Let's have a look at its meaning.

According to the *Oxford Dictionary*, the word vulnerable means: *Exposed to the possibility of being attacked or harmed, either physically or emotionally.*

Based on the above definition, if we were to suggest to someone that they *be vulnerable*, it would mean that we are telling them to allow themselves to be "Exposed to the possibility of being attacked or harmed, either physically or emotionally". I am sure this is not the intended suggestion.

In actual fact, the word vulnerable describes a person's status so that we can provide understanding and empathy accordingly. For example: At this point in time, s/he is quite vulnerable, let's be cautious with what we say to him/her. Or let's be mindful that things could be a bit sensitive at this point in time because s/he is in a vulnerable state.

When someone finally lets their walls and guards down, and 'becomes' vulnerable, it is good if s/he has the support of professionals such as a coach, counsellor, or a psychologist, because being vulnerable brings about a fragile feeling. It also leads to a feeling of disempowerment and violates somewhat the dignity of the individual.

My suggestion is to replace the phrase *be vulnerable* with '*be open, and be understood*" — this phrase simply reminds us to be open to those who care for us. Let the walls and guards down, *be open, and be understood by expressing true feelings and emotions,* so that our loved ones can understand how we truly feel.

Words have meanings and can trigger emotions into actions, so it is far better to use more positive words than negative words.

Therefore, "Be Open and Be Understood'" is my message. It is a simpler directive than be vulnerable. Just simply *be open, and be understood,* by letting others know how you truly feel so that they can offer appropriate assistance. This creates a much simpler and more inviting habit for connecting with others; it also helps to avoid complications and is definitely more self-empowering than being vulnerable, as there is no need for a support system if you are not vulnerable. A friend is all you need if you just *stay open and choose to be understood.*

If we all do this, we can start to inspire our circle of friends to do the same. It is also easier to care for our family and friends when they show their true emotions, rather than us having to guess how they truly feel and what they truly think.

Fear of Judgment

"Fear of judgment is what prevents us from being our authentic self and takes away our happiness."

— Linda Tomai Duong

It is only natural that we smile when we are happy and frown when we are sad. Do a happy dance when we feel victory and cry when we are hurt. These are our natural human responses and expressions, but as we grow older, we tend to hold back more and more, to the point that we no longer express how we truly feel.

Often, it is our own internalised fear of judgments by others that prevents us from sharing our emotions authentically. We fear that if we cry, it will show that we are weak. If we show excitement and joy, it will mean that we are *too* excited and *not cool*, which will cause us to lose the *'cool dude'* image that we are upholding, or being cautious not to be seen as showing off or something. Et cetera. For example, in some cultures, it is okay to shout to your friends: *"Hey, come over and have a look at my new car"* and it's okay to "toot your own horn", as we say in Australia, and your friends will run over to share your excitement, and even celebrate the occasion with you. Sharing our successes provides a chance to connect, to celebrate with people who love and care for us. It is a time to appreciate the 'fruits of our labour'.

In some other cultures though, it is not okay to do so. Such expressions and behaviours are considered boastful, and so from this point of view, we don't want to seem boastful, so we hide the excitement of our success. At times, we may even try hard to be modest, and don't want to show too much emotion and even refrain from sharing. So many little thoughts, so many worries and concerns that turn into fears and worries. This is in actual fact limiting ourselves in expressing ourselves fully and reducing the opportunities from connecting with others, and we do this without even realizing that we are doing it.

Isn't it time we cast away these, limitations, fears and concerns altogether?

We need to get back to our carefree-selves so that we can feel the freedom in expressions. It seems in our youth, we were to be able to show our true-selves more freely. As I reflect back on my own growing years — starting a new life at the age of 15 in a new country that I knew nothing about and where I didn't speak the language, was extremely challenging. Imagine if all you have seen of the world is your own little neighbourhood and all you've seen is black and white TV, black and white photos. You have never seen a world map or heard about the outside world much, and suddenly, you are 'teleported' to a totally different country where almost everything is opposite to what you know.

In Vietnam, everyone walk and drive on the right-hand side. In Australia, everyone walk the left-hand side. There, ladies and girls are to keep quiet, or speak softly and gently, never to speak up. There was no such subject as public speaking in school. Here, you practice to speak up and do show and tell at Pre-school age. And, even the funeral attire was opposite; white in Vietnam white and black in Australia, this was in 1985. I mean everything is operated in the *complete opposite way* than what I have learned, known, and grown up with.

Teenage years are already awkward enough, let alone adding the additional challenges of the extra awkwardness in having to learn a new language in a new country. Having to face new cultural practices that are the exact opposite to your own, as happens when you move from the Eastern world to the Western world, and having to make new friends with no local language skills was extremely challenging. The situation, simply gives you a 'speechless' teenager with extreme anxiety.

As the years went by, I grew up steadily with a more outgoing personality, and was soon feeling stronger physically, mentally and emotionally. I had also built good and strong family bonds as well as steadily increasing my circle of friends. When it was time for dating, and boyfriends, there were break-ups and broken hearts as inevitably just like other teenagers would experience; a few life learning curves. Fortunately, I was able to turn to my good friends and family for support.

I can still remember the days when I would call my best friend and burst into tears with inaudible mumbles. Or just simply pour my emotions out on to my brother or my best mate when I needed a more masculine energy kind of support to help me feel strong again. Yes, I was very lucky, I had male and female best friends. I could talk to my brothers as well as my sisters. There were also the times when I threw myself at my sister's shoulders and just burst into tears. We would sit there peeling the layers off, first came the downpour of tears, then the whining and complaining, then came the part where I was ready for the comforting words with empathy gestures. I was like a 'baby' again, feeling safe and cared for by people who cared and loved me.

At times like this, when we feel like we have failed and failed miserably, all we need is to have someone to turn to, whether it is family or friends, to reassure us with the message that: "No matter what happens, I am here for you." To let us know that there is always a safe place for us to fall into, regardless of how badly we have failed at something. However, this can only happen if we allow others in, to be our safety net for us, and we need to let go of the fear of judgment to do that.

I couldn't be more grateful to have such wonderful family and friends who I can turn to in times of need. I am deeply grateful too, for the close connections we have made that have resulted in strong bonds with each other over the years. However, I couldn't have taken the steps to allow all of this to happen if there weren't great role models for me to follow, to encourage me to be opened and seek the support I need while building the strong bonds and connections with others wherever I can, and whenever I can.

The two most prominent role models for me were Buddha and my mum. While I am referring to Buddha, I am cautious not to suggest any religious connotations regarding Buddhism. I am simply referring to the way that Buddha reached out and connected to others to find the answers he sought.

I was inspired by the way Buddha left his palace to reach out, to connect with the people outside of his comfortable, golden palace, in an effort to seek and understand the sufferings of life, and in which had led him on his journey to reach enlightenment. Similarly, in my mum's case, I was in awe of how she stayed open hearted and let her non-biological sister in, to connect with her and allowed herself to be helped and healed from the trauma of losing her mum at the tender age of eight.

As I grow older, reflecting on my mum's childhood story, I realise how lucky I was and how important it is to have a supportive environment in order to thrive and be happy. More importantly, I have also realised that we don't have to sit around to wait and yearn for this supportive environment. We can actually take the initiative and create the warm and loving environment for ourselves and for others. When you have established good friendships, even with teachers and neighbours, feeling the genuine love and care for each other, it is easy to return to your original-self.

Being a mother now, I am especially conscious of and aware that we need to teach our children to create this for themselves as they grow. If we all create a supportive environment for each other, we will all be happier.

"It only makes sense that when we need help, we are the one who needs to reach out, express it, and allow others in so that they can offer the help we need."

— Linda Tomai Duong

We must be the ones to initiate in seeking the help we need, in order for others to offer their support effectively. In the event that we cannot articulate those feelings by words, we can still express how we feel inside by writing it down, drawing it and/or painting it; as this will still help others to understand us. It is also a therapeutic way to release the heavy emotions so that we can lighten our hearts and clear our minds, which will essentially sets us free from the heavy emotions that we feel.

We need to remember the two things that we are entitled to; the first, is to express ourselves truthfully and respectfully as we wish, and the second, is to access happiness at any given moment should we choose to do so. In embracing these two entitlements, we have also opened the doors to be connecting with others in a more authentic, empathic and intimate way. Those that are truly worth loving will, in return, show us their love and care for us. It is only by us showing true emotions that we will receive true love in return.

There are also two basic feelings we experience as we go through the fragile moments in life; fear and love. We want to feel love and yet it is our fear that prevents us from receiving the love we need and deserve, because we fear the judgment of being needy if we express the need for love. We also fear that we may be perceived as not being strong enough, and that we are weak. Or that we have failed, and therefore we are not 'good enough', or not deserving of receiving the love we need. These are a few common examples of fears that prevent us from asking for the help and care that we need during those difficult times in our lives.

It is important to remember during these moments, that we are loved, and that we are entitled to our own feelings and emotions. Our family and friends will always love us if they have genuine care and love for us, otherwise we would not call them family and friends. So we can let go of the fear of being judged altogether. Otherwise fears can cause anxiety and downward spiral of negative emotions, and usually, anxiety stems from the feeling of lack of control. We simply cannot control what others think. My mum used to say: "*Their mouth belongs to them. They think what they think and say what they wish. Do not let that bother you. You cannot control what others want to say, so why let it bother you?"*

From this teaching, I have learned to let go of what others may think. What we each think is limited and based on the knowledge and experience we each have. It is also restricted by our own point of views and I have learned to tell myself: *"What matters is what I think of myself; everyone's opinion is different, and so is mine, which is different than theirs."*

It took many years of practice to let go of this fear of judgment by others but eventually I realised, it is not all that hard. *All it really required was for me to let and detach from the need to receive assurance and praise from others.*

When we worry about being judged, it is actually the opposite that is happening. Deep inside, we are actually yearning for reassurance and yearning to be praised that we are actually "good enough" while worrying that we are not. This is not the same kind of praise we are seeking as when we have done well at something but it is the comforting, reassuring, kind of praise that we secretly seek. The kind of praise that says: *"You're okay. You're good. You did well. Well done. It was not your fault."* Et cetera.

We simply want to feel safe, secure, and protected. We want to know that we are ultimately okay no matter what and that; "Others still care even when I've made mistakes," and that we are loved no matter what.

It is imperative for us to gain this clarity; between the fear of judgement that we hold and the yearn for love and care that we seek, and knowing that we are loved by our loved ones no matter what, so that we can accept, embrace, and love ourselves the way we are, *with all of our imperfections.* All we need to do is to give our friends and families the signs, signals, and permissions, to allow them in, to help us when we need help. It is okay to let go the worry of being judge by others.

If we can respectfully model this good feeling of being able to share and to connect with our authentic feelings, and to encourage the same from our friends, family, and community, we can establish a "culture" among our own circle of friends, just like the corporate companies establishing a work culture for their employees. We need to consciously choose to do it, to create such a culture that free us from the fear of judgment and to express ourselves authentically among each other.

Some cultures do this very naturally, particularly in the small closely knitted communities where people are dependent on each other's help and support. They let others help without resistance and ask for help at ease. If we all let go of the fear of being judged, it would help us all to build more cohesive communities and live a much happier environment.

"One of the most immediate ways to achieve happiness is to detach from the fear of judgment, and to accept, embrace and love ourselves the way we are, with all of our imperfections.

— Linda Tomai Duong

Self-Judgment versus Judgment from Others

One of the ways to lessen the fear of judgment is by being aware of the times when we are actually being self-judgmental, and yet we internalise it as being judged by others. For example, I have met some highly skilled professionals in their own country, such as a doctor, a lecturer, a professor and engineers whom have moved to Australia and, due to their lack of English language speaking skills, they have discounted their status to being "no one". Their comments were as follow: "We're professionals in our own country but now that we're here and we can't speak English well, we're just no one. No one knows who we are because we cannot speak English and we cannot find work." This group of individuals were being rather harsh on themselves. Just because they cannot speak the new language fluently does not mean that they had to discount themselves to "no one".

I was honoured to have the opportunity to speak to this group of high skilled individuals and reminded them that they are who they are, and that they still have the skills they came with, even though it is true that no one knows who they are or what they do unless they introduce themselves or educate others on their professional background, and the talents and skills they have.

If you have immigrated into a new country, it is very challenging to settle in a new country with minimal language skills. However, it will help you feel settled faster if you were to try and get out of your comfort zones to do some networking, and connect with others in the local community, and to take the opportunity to introduce yourself and letting others know who you are and what you do. It would also increases your opportunities for getting employment, and the most obvious benefit above all, is the chance to practice your English speaking skills as a bonus.

At times, we are our most critical judges when we are being too self-critical and too self-judgmental. We also confuse our thoughts when we internalise them to become the fear of being judged by others. This is when we need to be aware of the difference by checking in with our own thinking regularly, and by tuning into our thoughts to gain clarity with our own thought processes. This happens mostly because we have high standards of ourselves. We expect ourselves to perform at certain levels that are so high that we become harsh on ourselves without realising it, and this is also the time when we need to be aware of the difference between having high standards as opposed to being perfect.

There is a difference between striving for excellence and demanding perfection. Perfectionism is characterised by us striving for flawless performance and setting absolute high standards, accompanied by our self-critical evaluations. On top of that, we also have the concerns of others' evaluations upon us. All of these thoughts and concerns combined are what can cripple us from taking action due to the fear of 'not being good enough' to be perfect. It is due to this fear that many of us who are 'perfectionists' gave up before we even begin to try and achieve what we were meant to set out to accomplish.

All too often our minds are too busy and overcrowded with thoughts that prevent us from igniting that connection we have within ourselves and our ability to connect with our higher-self, which can cause us to listen to the wrong voice. A negative voice from our head that I call the "gremlin", which makes us feel doubtful and causes us to devalue ourselves. It can even be "delusional" too, and at times this voice can be so judgmental that it confuses us with having high standards, making us become self-critical. We need to recognise that there is a fine and yet crucial difference between the two. Otherwise, we fall victim to ourselves as we tend to listen to the wrong and negative voice rather than the self-empowering, inner voice that comes from our higher-self.

When we listen to the voice of criticisms and judgments, it confuses us with doubting thoughts, which spirals us into downward thought patterns such as, "Oh, for this to happen, I've got to be this good otherwise, forget it." Or: "I am not good enough to do that." Such negative self-talks put us into an idle position where we feel blocked and unable to move forward, towards our goals. It is the opposite of tuning into ourselves.

Whereas, if we are clear that we are aiming for a high standard, we could have thought patterns such as this: "My goal is to achieve level 10 on a scale of 10. For me to achieve that, I will need to be doing steps A, B and C, et cetera. Therefore, I need a plan of action to reach this goal. I am now only at the beginning, and that is okay. Given time and patience, I will get there." This thought pattern is simple and healthy. Yet, effective and empowering, as it moves us forward, rather than paralysing us on the spot, which happens when we are negative, self-judgmental and self-critical.

Having high standards is fantastic. It leads us to achieve great results. However, being self-critical does the exact opposite. When we are self-critical, we are harsh on ourselves, we take away our own credits and doubt our own abilities, which in the end cripples our true potential and preventing us from achieving best. It is imperative to have this clarity. When we listen to the wrong voice, we lose hope and give up, rather than persisting, taking actions, and giving things a go in life.

If you want to achieve something, just take small actionable steps — there's no need to keep waiting for things to be perfect before taking action. It is okay to take imperfect actions to move forward and evolve as you grow. Had I waited for things to be perfect before I took action, I wouldn't have achieved any of my dreams at all.

When you take action, each step of the way, it propels you to the next stage, and the next level, and as you go through the journey in life, you evolve. There is no perfection. What is perfect for one person is not to another. Everyone has different standards and different expectations. If you could let go of the self-judgmental thoughts and take actions, you are already on our way to achieving your goals. You just have to be your own best, operate from your own highest potential – knowing that 'you are enough' will make you feel much happier. This is why we need to make time for tuning into ourselves. To have the opportunity to truly reflect on our own thoughts, to be with our thought process in order to gain clarity, and then being able to hear our own true, intuitive voice rather than this self-critic voic. When we tune in, we can access our higher-self - our inner guidance, and feel our inner peace as we take the time to truly reflect in a balanced way, we can see that there are positives as well as negatives on the scale when making judgments, and that we all have strengths as well as weaknesses.

For every judgment we make of ourselves, we need to also give ourselves some credit and acknowledgements of the things we did well, to make it a balanced assessment. At the very least, we must acknowledge the challenges that we have faced and be kind to ourselves, and give ourselves more compassion and patience to overcome those challenges. We need to stop being so harsh on ourselves and instead, nurture ourselves more, and love ourselves more. Especially for women and mothers. We often tend to be our own worst judges and critics and, are not very forgiving of ourselves.

On the other hand, the person who doesn't have such high self-expectation would take action more easily and would have accomplished the goals sooner than the person that had higher self-expectation and were still procrastinating. Therefore, we must remember what is perfect for one person may not be so perfect for another and that there is no perfect. This is not meant to be a criticism towards perfectionism, yet in contrast, the purpose to comfort the 'perfectionists' and to encourage 'imperfect' actions, and to encourage all to taking action to move closer to the contentment state rather than being stuck at the judgmental state.

We cannot control the view that others have upon us, but we can control the view we have of ourselves and we need to be kind to ourselves rather than being too self-critical and too self-judgmental. As long as we have done our best, then we can ignore the rest of others' expectations.

Bridging the Gap for More Happiness

Another piece of advice we often hear is to "stay away from those who hold you back." Or "stay away from those who are not as positive as you are". I completely agree with this suggestion only if they have ill intentions. However, as for family and friends who do genuinely care for us but sometimes hold us back; it could simply be because they care too much for us.

They could be holding us back from the things we want to achieve because whatever new adventure we are about to embark on is too new, too risky, or too much cost involved either monetarily or otherwise, and simply too unfamiliar for them to support us. They do not see the vision we see, and simply don't feel as ready as we do, to take that next big step. Often, this is where the damage occurs, as it can cause the breakdown of the precious relationship.

Imagine this, you have found out that on the other side of the cliff, there is a hut full of treasure. All you have to do in preparation is train yourself so that you can leap over the cliff on the other side, to get to the treasure; something you know you have the talent and bravery to do. So, you begin the required training to prepare for this exciting opportunity. You get excited and tell your best friend, your husband, your wife, your father, your mother, et cetera, that you are about to take the risk and jump over the cliff to get to the treasure. "No! Don't do it," they scream, and hold you back. Not because they don't want you to get that treasure and achieve success. It is because they haven't done the training and the preparation that you have, and they fear for you. They do not have the bravery you have. They have many fears. Fear of failure, fear of the risk, fear that the opportunity may not even be real. Because they don't have your vision, they don't see or understand what you do. They simply do not have the insight and knowledge on the subject matter that you do. That is why they attempt to hold you back.

Their holding you back is sometimes out of protection, other times, out of their own insecurities and limiting beliefs, based upon their own life experiences. When this happens, they prevent you from achieving the success you desire and deserve. This is when some people say: "I wanted to do this and that, but my mum, dad, and husband or wife, didn't want me to do it or stopped me from doing it."

Clearly, the reason why you are told by the people who are more encouraging, to stay away from those who are not so supportive, is because they don't want you to lose your chances at the opportunities that have come your way to achieve success. There is a cost either way. However, when we break away from the people who care for us, it is such a shame. We lose a connection that is precious and has taken much time and effort to build. Patience and empathy is the only way to bridge and close this gap.

As much as our loved ones care for us, they may not feel as excited or as passionate as we do about our own new adventure.

They do not have the same information and vision as we do on our new project or journey. It is only natural that they feel overwhelmed with nervousness, anxiety and apprehension about what we want to do. Therefore, it is difficult for them to support us as they do not feel as passionate and enthusiastic about the opportunity as we do. For those who have ill intentions to stop us from achieving success, we usually can feel it deep inside, and can tell them apart from those who have genuine care and concerns for us.

If you believe that they have your best interests at heart and yet they are not showing supports, it only means that they are operating from a protective mode. They are worried that you may not succeed and want to prevent you from failing, and is mostly out of protection. It is such a shame though when this concern is mistaken as an ill-intention, so please be aware of such differences, should such a situation occur in your life.

It is almost like you are each on either side of a scale. One goes up, filled with enthusiasm, excitement and high energy while the other goes down, with the weight of fear and worry energy. These moments are frustrating but try to work at staying connected if you can, and understand that the other party has the best intentions for you, as this can help lessen your frustration.

One of the ways to bring the other party with you is to realign your energy level with his/hers, realign the level of excitement, wariness, confidence and trust to keep the connection close. If you can, slow down, pause, and take a big deep breath with your partner or supporter, and hold his/her hands if possible as this will help calm him/her down and offer reassurance.

In some circumstances where you have to make prompt decisions, that is when you will need to stay strong to make immediate decisions as required and follow your heart's desires, and then come back and bring the other person along with you, if you value their support. Patience is the key to staying connected.

Patience and empathy will help keep the precious bond between you both strong and keep the connection spirited.

It is almost like building a bridge between the two cliffs so that your valued supporter who was on the other side of the cliff can come over to your side and have his/her confidence renewed to support you on this new journey. It also helps at this time, to point out the other party's strengths so that s/he can realise and access that strength to provide the support you need.

Often people sacrifice their connections in their quest for success or to be right and, as a result, they end up feeling lonely, stressed and unhappy even after they have achieved much success.

It is much more valuable to have our loved ones supporting us. We would naturally feel much happier and more fulfilled when we have family, friends, and loved ones to cheer us on and support us, and to celebrate our achievements with us. That is when we have a *love-full and joy-full life.* It is a lot of work but the results make it all worthwhile.

Connecting with Your Other Half —
Happiness in Love and in Personal Relationships

"For meaningful connections to occur, your authentic self must be present. Only by showing true emotions can we receive true love."

— Linda Tomai Duong

Happiness in personal relationships and marriage needs to be in a book on its own. However, let's discuss briefly on each of the areas below. One thing is certain though, if we don't know our true selves, it is difficult and unfair that we expect our partners to understand us and make us happy. Below is a quick dialogue to illustrate the point:

Mrs.: "He just doesn't get it!"

Mr.: "No, you're the one who doesn't get it!"

She blames him, he blames her...! Who's right? Who's wrong?

Mrs.: "All he does is stuff his mouth and doesn't care a bit about anything!"

Mr.: "Well yeah, all she does is complain, complain, and complain! Criticise, criticise and criticise!"

Sounds familiar, doesn't it?

Life Coach: "Why do you complain and criticise him?"

Mrs.: "Because, when he eats, he doesn't care about his health!"

Life Coach: "Did you know that underneath the complaint was actually the worry and fear that she has about your health being compromised…?"

Mr.: "No, I thought she was just being picky and moody!"

Life Coach: "Do you two tell each other what you truly think?"

Mrs.: "No, I have just been busy worrying and saying out loud what worries me."

Mr.: "No, all I hear is her criticisms and complaints."

Life Coach: "Okay Mrs., would it be a good idea for you turn to face your husband now and tell him why you don't like it when he indulges in eating?"

Mrs.: "Look, honey… I know you like food and you enjoy eating and enjoy your buffets, but it worries me when I see you eat too much. I worry about your cholesterol levels. The minute I think that you're eating too much, it makes me feel worried and frustrated because I'm worried that you're damaging your health."

Mr.: "Oh, I thought you were just picking on me because you don't like my pot belly."

This is a quick example of how couples can get lost into daily bickering when they are not connecting on a deeper level.

Life is busy after having children, going to work, earning a living, and all that life throws at us. When we are being mindful of our partner's intention, knowing that each partner has the best interests of the other at heart, then a lot of the misunderstandings can be avoided and even eliminated.

Sometimes, even soulmates can be detached from each other, after years of marriage and being bombarded with the *busyness* of life. The only way to keep the relationship alive, fun and fulfilling is to stay connected with each other, such as having time out with each other. Date nights and time alone together can become vitally important to a couple's relationship. Time together creates opportunities for connection and re-connection between the couple, providing opportunities to continue nurturing the relationship; it's a time dedicated to checking in and ensuring that both parties are growing in the same direction.

It takes both sides to make the effort and to open up for authentic communication and connections. It is especially helpful for men to be aware that it is not always about solving problems but to tune-in and listen with your heart, and to be aware of how their partner feels, and to listen actively. Likewise, for women, it is important to stay calm, listen and share your feelings rather than to expect your partners to guess what's going on in your head, and be patient to see things through. Patience is a virtue and is priceless in relationships. No doubt, connecting is what keeps the relationship alive and provides the happiness for marriages.

There has been much emphasis on having self-connection in order to have self-love, to access our inner joy and inner peace, so that we can then ignite the love we have for others. When both parties are willing to work on achieving their own individual inner peace and inner joy, then the real 'happily forever after' scenario will be more likely to eventuate.

The reason why so many of us are in unhappy relationships, or have unhappy marriages is usually because one of the partners has found self-love and self-connection but the other person hasn't. Or while being together, one person may be connecting but the other person isn't because they are not being in the present moment. His/her mind is preoccupied with something else and s/he is not engaging in the conversation to be connecting with his/her partner.

Other times, it could be that neither of the individuals have found self-love, and self-connection, therefore, the couple can't feel the deeper connection that they seek in each other.

When you have done your part, and the other person is not yet where you are, all you can do is be patient and 'let it be' and continue to do what you do best. We can work on ourselves to inspire others to do the same, but *we cannot attain inner peace and inner joy for them.* For example, I have clients whom have asked me: "Can you coach my husband?" My answer is always: "Sorry, but I can't. I can coach you so that your actions inspire him, but I can't coach him until he asks for coaching himself, he has to be willing, so that he can have ownership of his own transformation, as the power is with him and in him." It is much more powerful and feels more empowering when we take charge of our own lives; at least whenever possible.

Each person needs to achieve their own inner peace, their own inner joy, their own ultimate happiness. It is their responsibility and their own choice. We cannot impose the action upon them. We can only inspire them to take action.

"Happiness is not about achievements alone. One of the ways to access happiness is when you connect with your partner authentically and deeply."

— Linda Tomai Duong

The following are attributes to a thriving relationship:

Self-love: As discussed earlier, we cannot give and receive love when we don't have self-love. We cannot feel the love that is coming towards us because of the blockage or resistance we have in accepting the love being presented to us. Either we don't feel deserving or we think that it is too good to be true and doubt it.

Self-belief and belief in others: This goes hand-in-hand with self-love, and helps with building trust and confidence both in ourselves and in others, which has an impact on the happiness of the relationship.

Trust: Trust is largely built through actions, respectful words and by being loyal to each other.

Respect: When I talk to different people, I notice that there seems to be variations, different perspectives and even diverse levels of respect. For example, in some Eastern cultures, people only relate respect to having high regard for their elders and people who have more seniority or a higher rank, whether this be through social status or in their working environment.

In the *Oxford Dictionary*, respect means *a feeling of deep admiration for someone or something elicited by their abilities, qualities or achievements.*

Whereas to me, respect entails more than the above definition. For example, we need to respect children for who they are. We need to respect each other for who we are. We also need to respect each other's space and privacy and will.

Often, partners that are in love with each other want to be with each other around the clock if possible. It is natural and should be that way because it says how much you want to be with the other person. In some instances, though, we need to respect each other's boundaries as well.

We may have good intentions to spend time with our partners and we want to be involved in everything they do and show them how much we love them. However, it is also important to respect their need for privacy, especially when they need time to be on their own to sort out their own emotions as they wish.

In maintaining a healthy relationship, it's important to actually communicate with each other verbally in ways that help to maintain the trust in the relationship. For example, it is much better to say: "Honey, I know you love me and want to be with me all the time. I do too. But I need some alone time to think about things and sort out my emotions." This is obvious and simple, yet without this clear communication and acknowledgement, both parties can begin to feel frustrated, which causes them to withdraw from the relationship and lessen the trust in each other, especially when each partner starting to guess what is going on with the other person.

Commitment: Knowing that when hardship hits, they have each other's backs.

Be nice and kind to each other: There is a difference between motivating each other to achieve a higher level and challenging each other, making each other feel less competent than the other.

Sad as it sounds but it does happen in couple relationships due to the power struggle stage in the relationship.

Patience for growth: Personal growth and growth within the relationship.

Growth in Personal Development: It helps the relationship to stay interesting and vibrant when we pursue personal growth. That way, the partners can consciously inspire each other to grow together. Growth gives us a sense of achievement and contributes to contentment.

Growth in the relationship: This is where we need patience most. Growing anything takes time. More so in a relationship. The first few years of being in love are always interesting as both partners are in love and so everything is seen with love in the eyes and nothing can come between the couple. However, after many years of being together, the level of tolerance for each other's habits decreases.

There is a saying; 'the seven-year itch in relationships' and there are many theories to it. There are also theories of human development based on seven-year cycles. All the more reason why we need to be patient with each other and also allow time for the relationship to grow as we grow individually. Hence, if both parties in the relationship participate in personal development activities, it helps to keep the couple growing together, rather than only one person seeking growth individually, which in some cases can end up causing the couple to grow apart from one another.

Seek to understand rather than fighting to win: Sometimes, we can get into a fight to prove a point of view on a certain topic. Other times, we just need reassurance that our complaint has been heard, and that our discomfort makes some kind of sense. It sounds like a small issue but really, a huge amount of friction in a relationship can be caused by the fear that our core emotional needs are not being taken seriously.

Sadly, the habit of arguing and proving a point only hurts our partner's feelings; and usually we don't realise that we are doing it. If we are to prove that they are wrong then we are right, which means we are smarter, which leaves the other person feeling unpleasant. If we're in love, we should be aiming to be on the same team, and our goal should be to resolve the issue, rather than to emerge victorious over the love of our life. So, instead of fighting to prove who is right and who is wrong, the best way is to try and understand each other's point of view, or core message.

For example, if your partner complains: "You are always home late or you spend too much time at work," it is very easy to react and say: "You do that too sometimes," or, "What's the problem with that? I am trying to work hard to earn more for us". It is better to take a conscious breath and think for a moment of the intention of the complaint. Perhaps, the real underlying issue is that your partner is missing you and wants to have more time and to feel more connected with you. That is why it is a very healthy habit to pause and think before we react whenever there is a complaint.

Set intentions for intimate and authentic connections: There's no doubt that when we make an effort on a daily basis to experience some sort of meaningful connection together, or create a fun memory with each other, it is the best thing we can do to strengthen a relationship, so enjoy this while you can before babies come along as they can keep parents too busy to connect with each other. Having said that, some couples manage the balance very well and they are able to make more meaningful and deeper connections after starting a family.

Starting a family can bring about conflict, and a mix of images, feelings, and emotions. Some people dread it and resent the hardship of being parents, others look forward to the deeper meaning of life that can be found in becoming parents.

Many relationships break up because we expect our partners to understand us and fix us. Happiness in relationships begins with us turning inwards first, because once we are satisfied with our own needs and feel okay within ourselves, then we can appreciate ourselves more and in turn have true appreciation for others as well. We will also be able to have a 'baggage-free' relationship; otherwise, the baggage will keep interfering and we will need to keep searching and searching from one relationship to another, looking for someone who can fill that empty space in our hearts for us, which is both unfair and unattainable for true happiness to appear in the relationship.

As long as we place the responsibility on the other person to fill up the emptiness in our heart - our own individual happiness, we will continue to disappoint ourselves, unless we take the responsibility to fill that emptiness of self-love. Loving ourselves will allow us to access true appreciation from within, not from others, our confident, self-content individual is what our partner can be proud of and appreciate us more, and together, both parties can contribute to a mutual, loving, fulfilling relationship.

Connection in Love and in Sexual Relationships

Connection in Love and in sexual relationships is pretty much the same as the chicken and egg question: 'Which came first, the chicken or the egg?" And so here, the question is: "which came first, the connection or the sex?" — In loving relationships, neither could exist without the other.

Although I am not a sex therapist or sex expert, and neither did I think about this topic at the age of 15 years old when I first embarked on the journey in searching for my happiness. However, it seems incomplete not to include such a topic as sexual connection when discussing how to achieve contentment and happiness in an intimate relationship.

To some people, when they hear the words 'sexual relationship', it immediately brings to mind erotic images and actions, and yet very quickly those images are replaced with the sense of feeling deflated when their reality does not match what they have imagined in their minds. At the same time, to others, sexual relationships bring about the romantic feelings of intimacy and deep connections with their partners.

Some people may have had sex from a one night stand and then realised that they have formed a connection with each other, and from there have gone on to establish a long-term relationship.

Whereas in a long term relationship situation, where a couple have been married for many years with grown up kids, and have been somewhat disconnected from each other, then they may ask; do you have sex to rekindle the connection or do you rebuild the connection before you can reignite the passion for sex? Just as in the chicken and egg situation, same as in a relationship; connection and sex, it can be impossible to say which of the two things existed first and which caused the other one.

However, for many who have experienced it, would agree that what ultimately leads to a great sexual relationship is the deep connections and compatibility; it's so much more than just attraction and physical action. It's about emotional and even spiritual connection. It's about feeling safe, and comfortable, and knowing you're in a position where you are completely trusting and can open your heart and soul to the other person, creating the deep loving feeling that feels like eternal love on earth, where you both feel like your souls are on fire. This is when you would say that connection is what has to come first in order to have a great sexual relationship with your partner.

In sexual relationships, connection begins when a little verbal foreplay, low lighting and soft music are all aspects of intimacy for both men and women.

While men may be listing their order of priorities slightly differently as to mood setting to help develop communication and a sexual relationship with a partner, it is no surprise at all, if you ask a more mature gentleman, to hear that he wants sex to help move him into a deeper connection, with all his emotional wants and needs met, and amazingly, even his spiritual connection with his soulful, intimate sharing. Even the words they use are more sophisticated and the thoughts are more philosophical as opposed to a man in his early twenties when he might discuss his view of sexual relationships.

Women, on the other hand, want that deeper connection the moment her man looks her in the eyes, the minute he calls her on the phone, and while he's opening the car door. Whatever her partner does, connections have to happen all the way before the bedroom door opens. A man must first penetrate right through to her heart and soul, which launches into her internal emotions, making her feel like she is the most beautiful, cherished goddess on earth, regardless of her age.

Ultimately, both men and women want the same thing —
Connection.

Both men and women want connections that are so deep and passions so electrifying, that making them feel like they are standing on an earthquake while the earth is shaking beneath their feet, with their hearts and souls on fire; where the intersection of two souls meets with such a deep kind of love that is suspended in time and in 'heaven'. That is ultimately the kind of connection that a man and a woman wants.

Without connection and when the two partners are not on the same page, the souls are deprived and the sexual relationship is not in existence. It is our souls that need the connection for our love to flourish, and relationships that flourish are ones that build life-long friendship among the partners themselves.

"Together, hearts and souls on fire; where the intersection of two souls meet, with such a deep kind of love that is suspended in time and in 'heaven' — that is the kind of connection that a man and a woman wants."

— Linda Tomai Duong

TIPS:

Connection and Happiness in Friendships —
Misunderstanding and Bullying

Back to friendships. Amazingly, sometimes best friends have deeper understanding for each other compared to some family members because there are no family dynamics and tensions, or conflicts of relations and/or complications.

Having said that, at times, misunderstandings are unavoidable. If we stay calm, remain patient and exercise empathy, often such a situation is what offers opportunities for both parties and the relationship to grow, once the issue is resolved. This is seen even in children's friendships, as in the following example that occurred in an incident in the school playground. A group of children were playing hand ball (a very popular game in Australia) in the school playground. *Ben was playing badly and should have been 'out' several times but the children involved were being aware and understanding of his emotional fluctuations and so they tried to put up with him. They let him continue to play. Finally, there came a moment when he was so clearly out and the other children had to expel him from the game. Instead of obliging by the rules, he got mad.

As soon as the children saw that he was angry they ran away, knowing that it was not fun when he got mad. Unfortunately,

*Kevin ran in the wrong direction and crossed over towards Ben. Ben immediately grabbed Kevin from behind with both arms and kicked his lower back several times.

Behaviour like this, is totally unacceptable! In many cases, the principal would have been called on and the issue would have become bigger. What followed is inspiring to share because the lesson came from an 11-year-old child. It demonstrates what can happen when we stay calm and that is the purpose of sharing this story.

What happened next was that Kevin, who understood Ben's temperament, decided that his action was not out of ill intent. He was just having an angry moment. Kevin *chose to be understanding* of Ben's bad behaviour, instead of being angry with him.

After the incident, when Ben realised Kevin was not angry at him, Ben wrote a very sincere apology letter to him, asking if they could remain friends and they have had no more conflicts between them since that day. In addition, from then on, Ben had fewer outbursts at school as he practiced modelling Kevin's calmer way of being. He began to confide in Kevin and consulted him for support when he needed it. Since then, Ben became a loyal friend of Kevin's.

As we can see, even an 11-year-old child can demonstrate that when we turn inwards and connect to our feelings and other's feelings, we became more intuitive and more understanding in dealing with other people's emotional challenges as well as his own.

This story has shown that paying attention to the emotions of those around us helps everyone to live together more harmoniously, and it can only happen if we allow ourselves to connect to each other authentically.

I share this story because I hear so many stories about bullying among children in school. Of course, I understand that it is a very complicated area to deal with because bullying is such a LARGE area in a very W I D E range of issues under a very B I G umbrella of misbehaving behaviours.

This story is by no means addressing the bullying behaviour adequately. I am aware of the pain and the complications bullying can bring. I am also more than aware that sometimes, we take away our own happiness too easily when we get tangled in the issues of bullying when, in fact, we can actually resolve it and make it smaller rather than making it more complicated. Not all cases are as bad. It is my wish that we teach our children to feel, and learn to show more compassion for each other and help them find better ways to resolve conflict as they are learning to navigate the world around them. We can teach our children to tune in or pay attention to their feelings and emotions as well as their own, and learn to understand each other more. We can teach our children to be more emotionally intelligent.

We all can help our children learn to understand themselves first and then understand each other. With respect, sincerity and open heartedness, we might even be able to turn a bully into a friend as proven in the above case and many other cases that I have heard and witnessed when the issues are addressed and resolved early on with compassion.

We need to demonstrate to our children that we can make what looks like bullying issues smaller and resolve it calmly, and they too will learn how to do so from us modelling it.

Generally, children can develop deep compassion if they are shown how to. Compassion is what will help children grow into more connected individuals and that will allow them to achieve happiness more easily.

Like many things in friendship, it requires team work. In order to resolve conflicts, both parties must be willing to listen, communicate openly and sincerely without fear of judgment and, last but not least, be committed to staying connected to clear the misunderstanding in order to keep the friendship going.

"A lone wolf is not as powerful as in a pack!"

Linda Tomai Duong

"We need to allow others in, and allow them to be our safety net for us."

Linda Tomai Duong

"One of the most immediate ways to achieve happiness is for us to let go of the fear of judgment, and to accept, embrace and love ourselves the way we are, with all of our imperfections."

Linda Tomai Duong

"If we all create a supportive environment for each other, we will all be happier."

Linda Tomai Duong

"Together, with hearts and souls on fire; where the intersection of two souls meet, with such a deep kind of love that is suspended in time and in 'heaven' — that is the kind of connection that a man and a woman wants."

Linda Tomai Duong

Chapter 8

Happiness in Finance through Personal Success

"It is not how much we earn but the meaning of our earning that brings us happiness."

— Linda Tomai Duong

Having the basics of finance in place frees us up from worrying thoughts and helps us to feel more at peace to connect with others.

When we talk about connection for success, naturally the statement: "It's not what you know but who you know" comes to mind. If that is the way to success and happiness, then why is it that there are so many who have achieved financial success and yet are still not happy? What is the missing piece in the success puzzle that is required for happiness to be present...?

Connection with Your Passion for Career Success and Happiness

So many people are not happy doing what they do. Some people are earning very well but are not entirely happy. Others may not earn as much, yet they are happy and feel fulfilled.

Are you happy with what you do? If not, ask yourself, why is it that I am not happy doing what I am doing?

Most of the time, the answer is "This is not my passion" or "This is not what I dream of doing".

So, here are some focus questions we need to answer to discover the secret to our happiness at work:

What do you enjoy doing and feel passionate about?

What can you do well naturally?

Why do you do what you do?

What value does it serve for you to do what you do?

What areas do people normally ask your help for?

If money was not an issue, what would you like to do right now?

Here are some sample answers:

I am a garbage collector = What.

To keep the community germ-free = Value.

To keep the community clean so that people can be free of germs, illnesses and diseases = Passion.

To contribute to the health of all humans and animals and all beings = Purpose/Contribution.

I will invent robots and machines that can help clear up landfills = Dreams.

I often think that apart from the air force soldiers, fire fighters, navy, paramedics, and police, garbage-men are also the important contributors. However, reality is, we cannot live a fulfilled life without one another. Whatever job you do, whoever you are, you are important. We all contribute to this universe and to each other, directly or indirectly. That is the invisible connection we all have with each other.

If you are the farmer, you are the one who keep us fed so we don't go hungry. If you are the salesperson, you brings us more joy through the products we purchase. If you are a doctor or nurse, you save our lives; if you are a teacher, you help raise the next generation of leaders, the next presidents or the next prime ministers. If you are the garbage-man, you keep our environment clean, free of germs and free of diseases.

All jobs are important and have their place in terms of significance and importance in society. Every job, every person serves a purpose in life, whether we feel the job we are doing is our purpose or not.

For example, a nurse will tell you that her purpose in life is to help the sick, injured, and wounded, and that, she couldn't see herself doing any other job, while someone else would say: "I could never be a nurse. I can't work with seeing blood!"

Ultimately, what we are seeking is a job that brings out our natural skills or our innate talents which help us build on as our passion and connect us to the job deeply. This enables us to feel enjoyment on the job, and allows us to appreciate the meaning and value the job holds. It is when we see the job as a means to contribute to others that we can say we've found the job that gives us our sense of purpose in life.

Picture yourself at 80, or 90 years old. You are happy, feeling content with life, and then imagine you are writing your own eulogy. What would you want to be remembered for? What matters to you most? What would you do if you knew it was impossible to fail?

Basically to find your purpose in life is to choose a job that is in line with your values, and allows you to enjoy the journey and to bring out the passion in you as your work contributes to other's wellbeing, and ultimately lets you dream on and grow as you journey through life.

At times, we see people walk away from their high paying jobs after years of studying and qualifying for the job. This is because they cannot find the connection between the job and their passion. Either the job does not match their natural talent or they don't see the value the job offers others. They don't feel it is their 'calling' to be doing that particular job.

Most of us have a particular interest and 'gift'. If and when we are given the opportunity to nurture that interest to become our passion, strength, and talent, for us to realise that it is a gift that we can use to serve others, which in turn becomes our passion and purpose in life.

I believe that we all have a purpose in life. We all have a calling that speaks to our hearts and that is what we refer to as our "purpose on earth".

Some people see it clearly and sooner while others take longer to see it. If you keep seeking inwards, paying attention to what you do well naturally, and what makes you feel happy, and enjoy doing, and continue to build on that with intuitive feelings, then eventually you will see the value it brings to others, and once you have embraced it, it will become your passion and purpose. Once you have found your passion and purpose, you will feel like a weight has been lifted from your shoulders and elated with joy.

You will feel more joy and be at peace doing your job and, most importantly, you will feel a sense of connection to the world, in serving your purpose in life. Once you have found that feeling, it does not feel like a job regardless how hard you work, you are just living in connection with it, and you are in your element, and things seem to be smoother and you will feel in harmony with yourself. Whatever you do, it is the *meaning* that connects you to the job.

It is the meaning of what we do that connects us all to each other. Therefore, I see that we all have a purposeful job and we all serve a purpose in life. It is just a matter of us finding the alignment of the value we each hold individually and reflecting on the value the job offers others, so that we see it as our purpose in life.

"When you lead a life that has deep connection to your work and live with passion, you are living your life on purpose."

— Linda Tomai Duong

Take a Different Path, Reach Out and Connect

When things don't work out as planned, it is okay to take a different path. We have to be able to detach and let go of what's not working or not serving us and make room for bigger and better things to come.

When we offer our passion as a service or product, it will allow us to feel more in-tune with ourselves, more in-tune with our life purpose and thus we feel more fulfilled.

To transition from a job that is only income earning to a passionate, soulful, life purpose serving kind of job, takes time. It takes testing and requires patience. Sometimes it is just a matter of connecting with the right people or to the right channels at the right time. So this is when we say: "It's about whom you know," so that we can gain access to the right guidance, tips and help needed for this new journey.

You might want to start by doing it as an on-the-side-hobby kind of job and let it build so that you can test and confirm, that is what you want to do before you quit your full-time job to maintain your financial security and stability. Others will know what it is that they need to do to fulfil their wishes and that 'tomorrow might never come' so, they don't have two minds about it. They can just quit the job they don't enjoy and pick things up and go for it. Either way is fine.

Do what your heart tells you. If you are clear on what you need to do to achieve your dream job then give yourself the permission to do it.

However, there is a difference between a hobby and a passion; hobbies can turn into a passion, but a mere hobby won't inspire the drive and determination and fight necessary to do something for a living and that is the difference.

A hobby is something that we love to do in our 'spare' time that makes us feel good and relaxed. Something we can 'escape' to and often with ease and without having to fight for it as we do when we are passionate about our work.

A passionate we work hard for, on the other hand, ignites stronger emotions. It is not exactly relaxing in terms of easiness. In fact, your passion draws you to it so much that you can't be separated from it. It goes with you wherever you go. It's on your mind 24/7. It will come even in your sleep, and sometimes even comes in between you and your partner or family if you are not balancing it well.

Passion injects itself into your life, whether you have time for it or not. For example, you might be sleeping and suddenly, Ding! Not the clock or the mobile phone alarm bell but your mind, your creative mind just wakes up, filled with ideas as if it has a bell of its own. Sometimes, my brain wakes me up at 3:00am whether I like it or not, whether I am tired or not, and whether it is planned or unplanned. Inspiration just creeps in whenever it feels like it!

I am not even in control of it.

That is when you know that it is passion. It's those times when all your friends and family are celebrating public holidays, having extra days off with long weekends, but you, on the other hand, are trying to make good use of the spare time by crazily working on your project. That is passion and with a bit of craziness too. Crazy as it sounds, it's true. That is why balancing your work with family and downtime is a good reminder.

We think of a passion as something we love, with devotion and obsession. Yes, it is with devotion and obsession and often with a price too. The price could be monetary, time, and/or efforts involved. Not many people are willing to pay the price and therefore they do not go on full force forward to ignite that passion and to take the action required to succeed.

When trying new things, finding people who have travelled that path before you helps a great deal. It really helps if you can find the right person that is willing to share their experience, that way you can see whether or not the path that they took is also the path you want to take. At the same time, be mindful that each individual has their own journey and can experience different things and can have different levels of achievement. So, we need to be mindful of our own journeys.

Sometimes, when you have connect to the right experts in your field, you could say that connection equals knowledge if used well. To gain the maximum benefit, make the most out of networking opportunities as that is when and where you can reach out and connect with industry peers and experts. You can connect either in person or through the internet, and if you are proactive at reaching out to connect sincerely, you will see the benefits for both parties.

"Give it a Go! Allow Yourself. Connect with Your Passions!"

When you take a new path, it doesn't mean that you have to think of something new and completely unseen or different. As long as it is something you are passionate about, even if it is something that has been done before, it does not matter. It is your style, your personal touch that creates your signature style and that will produce something that is uniquely yours.

Your personal touch, your tone of voice, your passion, and the way you present it, is definitely different than others whom are offering the same thing. Hence, there are no worries or concerns about offering the same product or services. No one can do the same as you even if there are two people who provide the same product or service. So the next time you have an idea and worry that others have already done it, just ignore that worry and go for it. The least you can do is give yourself a chance to have a go at what you're passionate about. Allow it to happen. It's only when you allow yourself that you can immerse yourself in your passion which then enables you to produce your special service or product that is uniquely yours — with your taste, your style, and your vision with its benefits for clients. This is when you allow your vision and mission come to life and your creative ideas to flow.

For example, if you are someone who loves dogs, you could start by offering dog walking, dog sitting, dog grooming, dog minding services, even a dog boarding kennel. The first step is to ignore the self-judgmental thoughts inside your head that say, "Maybe it's not a good idea", "Someone's already doing it" or "How do I even start?" The first and most important thing to do is to stay focused on the idea, and let the idea grow, then let your creative mind continue to take that idea to the next level. You can even create the following merchandise for dogs such as; tutus (for the girls), vests (for the boys), jewellery and leather boots for both. All that are specially made for each type of dogs, and of course you can even create it with your own branding labels on them.

If you find that this is the idea you will take on, please be sure to connect with me and let know how you go. I would love to hear from you.

"Simply focus on connecting to the passion you have for the work you do, in and of itself. When you do that, it will give you the drive to come up with creative ways to do the job well."

— Linda Tomai Duong

When I focus on the passion itself; being with the dog and doing everything with the dog, I become connected to the joy it brings. There is no time and space in my head for negative thoughts, and the 'gremlin' in my head can't challenge me. It has no space, no chance as I am too busy thinking about my passion and being busy with the creative ideas it brings, rather than letting negative thoughts creep in.

Once you shut the 'gremlin' with negative backchat out, you will be able to create things with a carefree mind. Creativity comes when you love what you do. Once you allow yourself to nurture that passion, your creativity will flow naturally.

Believe in Yourself — See Your Own Value

Believe in yourself. When you have an idea, an invention, or vision, just have trust and believe in yourself. Write the idea down, work on it and keep at it until you can achieve the result you desire.

No need to tell anybody before you action the idea unless you require support, and if you do require support, be strong and hold on to your original idea. This is because others might not see what you see in your creative mind and the vision have. Often they try to help and offer suggestions but sometimes that can alter your original view or plan.

When it comes to charging for your services, apart from the market/industry price, be confident on the fee you want to charge or the amount you want be paid for your work. 'Own it'. There is no need to wait for someone to tell you how good you are or how valuable your services are. You can give it the value you think your work deserves. Think of the value that the client will benefit from. The peace of mind they will receive is priceless.

When we value our work, it comes with pride and confidence. That is when the client will see the value we deserve. If you think that you are just dog-sitting, you will pay yourself a very small fee, but if you think of the peace of mind that you provide the dog owners, you will pay yourself a better fee. Think of the ultimate benefits that you are providing, that will guide you to formulate a fair fee for both you and your clients.

Imagine the guilt-free feeling you are offering to the dog owner who has to stay back for a meeting and cannot walk their dog, or how much relief you can provide to them when they are going on business trips and have no one to attend to their dogs, and when they want to go on holidays but where they go doesn't allow dogs and so they can't take the dog along with them. Most people will pay for what is valuable to them. So focus on the quality of your service offering, rather than making the price cheap with lower quality services.

"Allowing yourself to do what you love is the first step in achieving your dream and getting closer to your life purpose."

— Linda Tomai Duong

Many people refrain from doing the things that they love doing for many years, for many reasons. Our parents' and grandparents' time was different. They went through the war time and it was all about function and survival. Therefore, not all of them had the luxury to choose a profession based on their passions and dreams. In fact, many of them didn't have time and space in their minds to be thinking about passions, other than providing for the family, surviving and functioning.

That was the model that was passed on to us; that our jobs were to serve the function of survival first. Therefore, the majority of us were told to study and get jobs that come with good pays, rather than focusing on our passions and what we enjoy doing. However, things are different now, we have evolved, and are blessed to a lot more resources than the past generations do. We are able to choose a job that serves our functional needs as well as satisfying our wishes of having a passion and serving our purpose, while also making a living.

Not everyone's job is in line with their values and passion, and if you're still seeking and finding your way to a job that brings out your passion, be patient as it will come. In the meantime, finding your way to nurture even the smallest thing that you enjoy doing is a good beginning. Be it as simple as cooking, knitting, sewing, drawing, painting, leatherwork, woodwork, gardening, horse riding, skating, surfing, bush walking, or hiking et cetera. Anything at all. Anything that sparks your interest, it will eventually bring out your innate passion and creativity. Anything that you enjoy can ignite old and new passions in you. You will be surprised at how much joy and value it adds to your daily life if you start to allow a hobby to come back into your life in even the smallest way.

Another way to ignite your passion is to imagine you have won the jackpot lottery of $55 million dollars. Now you have all the time you need to do something you really like doing, to pass your time. Ask yourself: "What would I choose to do with my time?" Whatever you choose is a good indication of what your passion is. It may change and that is okay, but it is a good start to think of it in this way. When you have no financial constraints, what would you create? Enjoy answering this question and let your imagination run free.

Regardless of age, anyone can activate the passion they have inside. A quick example is an eight-year-old girl who says she loves animals, and that she wants to grow up with a big house full of pets. This is her love and her passion. Upon hearing this, a neighbour who goes on frequent short holidays throughout the year, decides to give her the job of feeding her pets; two gold fish and a cat, once a day and clean up the cat's litter as well. Instead of engaging a commercial service, which would have cost the neighbour a higher fee, she gave the job to this young, but very capable girl.

The neighbour saved some money by avoiding the high commercial fees. The girl gained some pocket money but, most importantly, she had the opportunity to test out whether or not she could really handle the chores that came with having pets. It was definitely a win-win situation. However, if the neighbour did not know about the girl's passion, she wouldn't have known to offer her the job.

It is good to be open, to communicate, connect, and let others know what you want to do in order for them to help you achieve your goal. No need to be shy or to worry. Young people may not be able to do it on their own, so adults can help and we need to be the ones to guide our children to learn to communicate and articulate their thoughts, emotions and passions, and learn to connect with others. Connecting openly works for all ages and often both parties gain.

This simple story reminds me of two things. The first is to always share your passions, connect, connect and connect, so that others can help you achieve your dreams. Always connect with others. The second thing is to be aware of your thoughts so that you can be in tune with your passion, and know when and how to articulate it so that others can help bring your passions and dreams to life.

Unlike the previous generations, our children now have the resources and opportunities to do much more and have more freedom than those in the past. They can learn to be aware and understand what they like to do purposefully, learning to be aware of their hobbies and passions as they grow into adulthood.

It is wonderful to be able to live and grow with your passions and dreams. No more searching and chasing for it until a midlife crisis hits to be asking "What is my dream?" Life is much better and happier to be able to build on the many dreams children have as they grow.

As life goes on, children grow and evolve. Their thoughts, development, and passions will most likely change, but that does not matter. What matters is that they are actually following their hearts and doing what they love as they grow up, and *it affirms to them that: "I can do what I love and am passionate about. And I live with my passions as I grow." This is my message for the next generation.*

I was very fortunate to do this my whole life. When I was five years old my dream was to make beautiful dresses. At seven years of age, my dream was to see the world. At age 10 I dreamt of being a teacher. When I was 15 all I wanted was to be an artist. After becoming a mum, I built and achieved even more dreams.

I had the privilege to travel the world when I worked as a travel consultant in 1991, then I opened a bridal boutique offering personalised designed dresses in 2001. After having children, I worked on a very causal basis as a casual part-time preschool teacher in 2012. I have achieved all of these three early childhood dreams. After that, I went on and studied visual arts, which gave me the opportunity to participate in exhibitions and win prizes. In 2016, my self-portrait was awarded as one of the finalists for the Women's Art Prize. From there, I realised that there are no limits to dreams. I wanted to help others to achieve their dreams too, so I travelled to America to train as a Life Coach and since then have become a Motivational and Inspirational Speaker and co-authored a book entitled; *If I can, You can — Winner's Edition*; my chapter was *Follow Yours Dreams*, and now I've written this book. Dreams are unlimited.

"You can achieve as many dreams as you want!" This is the ultimate message we want our children to experience and grow up with.

— Linda Tomai Duong

Regardless of age, both children and adults can learn that we can achieve our dreams more easily by connecting with ourselves and with other people. It is a fundamental and empowering thing to do. If you want to offer your products or services, *once ready, just announce it, believe in yourself and connect with others; and let things happen.*

You will experience small incremental steps that will help you propel to the next steps. Other times you may even experience pivotal steps that have you bounce and leap to reach your goals much faster than you would if you were to do it all on your own.

This goes back to the point that connections are as valuable as knowledge if used well. Not to mention that it also leads to attaining contentment and happiness while we connect with other like-minded people.

If you don't know what your passion is, just try doing different things, different activities, until you find something you really enjoy doing, then share it, and announce it, so that others can support you on your journey.

Friends and family are our greatest supporters. Everything starts with our friends' and family's support. I don't mean that you should exploit your relationships and turn them into your customers. What I am referring to is connection, emotional, and mental support.

If they don't know what you're doing, they simply cannot support you. Sometimes, emotional and mental support is more important than anything when you embark on a new journey. They may have friends that would be a great fit for you to connect with. Someone always needs something. Simply tell your friends what you can offer as friends are the best source for referrals if you have established great respects for each other. It is all about connections and connecting authentically and sincerely with each other so that we can help each other out.

Happiness in Your Job and Having Life Balance

Happiness in your job is when you have found what you love doing, and can be paid to do what you love, then, what you do is what represents you. That way, there is no separation between the person (you) at work, and the person (you) out of work. They are the same person. Therefore, there is no work-life balance. There is only *life balance.*

Life balance is essential and central to our happiness. Eat well, rest well, drink lots of water as most of our body is made up of water. It is healthy to have about two litres of water a day. You cannot be happy when you are dehydrated with a headache and getting all grumpy. You cannot achieve optimum work performance if you are not fit and well. So, physical exercise should be considered as part of your work day to develop optimum health, and therefore the focus should be on *health and life balance.*

One of the main life balance disruptors is stress. In business, finance is what causes stress fastest. Always be mindful of your choices to avoid stress as much as possible.

For example, I once engaged a freelancer to do a job. Upon agreeing with the quoted price, she took up the job. Some weeks had gone by and she realised that the job would take her longer than what she had quoted. Without consulting me and/or seeking my agreement, she issued an additional invoice. This was clearly not on. Of course, I refused to pay the extra invoice and contacted my appropriate lawyer, who had prepared to contact an overseas lawyer should we proceed ahead, as it was an international dealing.

I was upset at first and sought all the advice I needed and it was clearly a winning case for me, should I choose to proceed. However, I paused and considered, deciding it was not worth my time and energy. I refused to waste my precious time and energy to engage in such tasks that can easily take away my inner peace. I chose a different path of thinking. Rather than thinking winning or losing, I turned to my parents' great model, and thought instead from the place of the generosity of the heart.

She obviously needed the extra payment, and even though I was running on a strict cash flow constraint, I still decided to pay the extra invoice, and I had the right to refuse to pay the additional invoice because I had never agreed to it. However, either way, to dispute it or to go through with it and win it, it still would have taken up my time and energy and the case would have stolen my inner peace from me. By detaching myself from winning and losing mentality, and operate from the place of abundance, I was able to sustain my inner peace and the harmony in my work flow. Of course, not all cases are dealt with in this exact same manner, and each case is dealt with differently. In this case, I chose to operate from a place of abundance rather than scarcity. As soon as I removed the ego thinking pattern of winning or losing, I was able to regain my inner peace.

I have learned that in life, we lose here and we gain there. We give when we can and receive when we need to. It is a circle of love and humanity.

What I am sharing here is to remind us all NOT to be taken away from our own inner peace so easily, and not to let financial stress disrupt our happiness flow. We need to be mindful where we invest time and energy, which in some cases is more precious than financial gain, because we can always earn more money when we retain our energy, health and happiness. Of course, I am aware that if it has to do with significant issues of integrity, then we must make it clear that all judgments must be made and taken more seriously. However, please note that fighting for integrity is different than fighting because of our egocentric self. We need to be mindful and choose our battles and, most importantly, preserve our positive energy, to maintain our harmony and happiness wherever, and whenever we can.

TIP:

How much money would you like to earn or have in the bank? How much would you say is enough for you? Do you need to have a million dollars before you can be happy? Okay, maybe that's not so for everyone.

For many people, having a steady income that provides enough for a place to call 'home sweet home', a place where we can lay our heads at night, feeling safe and secure, is the foundation of happiness. This sense of security and stability is what leads to a worry-free mind, allowing us to be present, to be able feel settled in order to connect with others. It opens up ways to feel inner joy, inner peace, and on to true contentment and happiness.

Making a Large Number Smaller

The first step towards happiness in financial goal setting is knowing what you need. If you know the least amount you need, as well as the largest amount you wish to attain, then it gives you a very clear goal to work with.

It helps to know your desired amount of income. Having a specific number in your mind makes for a great motivator. It is also a great idea to have an ideal goal and a realistic goal. For example, the realistic goal is to earn $50,000 in the first year and the ideal goal is $100,000. Next comes the secret of making this amount achievable.

Let's say your goal was to earn $100,000 in a year.

Take that $100,000 and divide it into 52 weeks, you need to earn $1,923 per week.

Take this weekly goal of $1,923 and say divide that into a 40-hour work week, then you need to earn $48 per hour.

*You can divide the desire earning amount in to however many hours you would like to work.

Now you know that you need to achieve an average of $48 per hour, for a 40-hour week, to achieve $100,000 a year. This makes your goal clear, specific, measurable, and achievable. However, the first step of breaking the number down is crucial as it shrinks the large and overwhelming numbers into a much smaller number, making it much easier to achieve.

If your hourly pay is not this amount, you can create options to help increase the earning. You can cross-sell, upsell and add extra services to help you achieve your goal. By knowing your goal so specifically, you can become creative in finding ways to achieve it.

Here are some funny, out of order kinds of ideas to trigger your creative mind into thinking of ways to earn extra money if you were starting out earning:

Art for sale

Babysitting

Bike cycling to do deliveries such as newspaper, pizza, take-away orders

Boat model making

Blogging

Cat minding

Cookies — homemade orders for cafes

Cooks, chefs

Crochet personal items for special orders/Crochet teaching

Decluttering services

Dog walking

Drop and pick up dry cleaning

Drop and pick up kids before and after school for busy professionals

Editing

Embroider personal items for special orders/Embroidery teaching

Fishing for dinner and save the spending

Fish and chips take away sales assistance

Gardening services

Gutter cleaning

Home cleaning

Ice-cream selling

Ice-skating coaching

Juggling/busking

Key cutting

Kimchi selling — homemade orders for friends, neighbours and local restaurants

Kitchen hand

Kite selling

Knitting personal items for special orders/Knitting teaching

Lamp selling/Lampshade creation for special personal orders

Lemonade stalls

Lollipop selling

Moussaka selling — homemade orders for friends, neighbours and local restaurants

Noodle selling — homemade orders for friends, neighbours and local restaurants

Novel writing

Orange selling — work at fruit shops

Oyster farming, oyster selling at a fish market

Pizza delivery, pizza chef

Packing jobs at the big department stores

Quantum physics writing

Quilt-making classes

Résumé assistance

Racquet fixing — restringing

Social media profiling

Shoe selling

Sandbox selling — the wooden ones for kids to play in as well as the digital ones

Transcribing

Technology assistance

Umbrella selling

Uniform repairs

Vegetable growing to save on spending

Vegan meals — homemade orders for friends, neighbours and local cafes

Waffle selling — homemade orders for friends, neighbours and local cafes

Walking and shopping assistance for the community's seniors

Xylophone teaching, performing

Yacht cleaning services

Zucchini growing and selling

Zodiac and star sign reading

The above list is just for a bit of out of the order kind of creative fun, and the main idea is to take your mind away from your usual thoughts and comfort zones, as this is the safest way to test and to try think out of our comfort areas, and if it had triggered a solution then it has served its purpose in igniting your creative mind, and you can build on more ideas from here.

Goal Setting versus Limitations

Often people have goals but they are lost for directions before they even begin the journey. Imagine that your ultimate goal is to climb to the peak of a mountain, and when you stand at the bottom and look up to the mountain's peak, it can appear too overwhelming to even begin the first step. This is why many people quit before they even begin.

The most common self-dialogue is: "This is impossible!", "I can't do this", and "This is way too hard!"

Instead, *imagine that you are already on top, at the peak of the mountain looking down.* Now you will find that, you have a better view of the route you need to take in order to reach your goal. This will give you courage as well as a mind map to plan your journey.

It makes logical sense to begin with the end goal in mind in order to achieve better results. Using the power of imagination and visualisation will take you to your future goal and provide insights for your current self as to how to achieve what you want to achieve in the way that you need to achieve it. This approach is an effective and mindful way of achieving goals. You get to design how to manage your own journey.

Looking from the top down allows CEOs and executives not only to get to see how their team is performing but also which pathway they need to use, to lead their team towards success, as individuals and as a team, and ultimately as a company. They are able to design their journey, incorporating their own style, system, and method into creating the culture they desire for their team, as well as envisioning their ideal work environment along the way. They can even inject fun into the journey by having better connections with their staff and employees.

For individuals, with an end goal in mind, you will have clarity around your goal and what you want to achieve, and therefore it helps with planning and measuring your achievements and success along the way. If the path you are taking is no longer serving your purpose, you can choose to take another path to make your journey more enjoyable and meaningful. It is okay to take a different path. You just need to *allow yourself* to do that. Don't wait for other people's approval. If it feels right for you, just do it!

"Why Not Me?"

Many people have said to me: "I could have written that book" or "I could have been that person on TV!" So why didn't they? It's because they never thought that they could be that person until they saw that other person achieve it. *You can be that person*, provided you let yourself be, instead of asking *"Why Not Me?"* afterwards.

Let's say you are going to a job interview where they have shortlisted you from 500 applicants. You have done your research and you are pretty sure that you meet all of the company's criteria. There is only one thing left you need to do: *You need to allow yourself to be that person.*

At this final stage of the interview, many people start worrying about whether they are good enough with thoughts like: "Am I going to be the one?" "I hope I am good enough. What if the other applicant is better than me?" Instead of thinking "I am the one!" They start to compare themselves to the other finalists and worry about their chances.

It is much better if you start thinking: "I am the one for the job" or "I am the one they need". With such positive, affirming thoughts in mind, you will be able to cast away your nerves and step up from the competition, which helps to ignore the other finalists' threads. This thought pattern will also allow you to focus on connecting with the interviewers much better.

This is not to suggest that you behave with any arrogance but is instead to help you position your mind to be laser focus, and not allowing chances for distracting negative thoughts. It is also much better to fill your mind with images of how you would perform on the job as if you are already employed, and imagining how you will relate to the staff and the team members there.

If you could treat it as your orientation meeting or something similar, it will lessen the intense nerves of this final stage of the interview. It will also create an instinctive feeling that enable you to connect with the interviewers at a very different level than if you were sitting there being nervous, thinking: "Am I going to be the one they choose?" You will be less anxious and will be calmer. So, the next time you are attending an interview, just *think and allow yourself to be THAT person, and chances are, you will be.*

Remember, the interviewers want you to be that person too, as once the prospective employee is chosen, they can close the process, to save time on interviewing so many more people. It is the non-verbal connection that makes the difference from one candidate to another. The way we connect with another person is something that cannot be written down on a résumé. So, the next time you're attending an interview, simply connect, connect, connect, and believe in yourself, and start connecting with the thought that: "*I am the one they're searching for; I am that person*" — embrace the fact that we can *allow* ourselves to be that person, and your responses will reflect differently as you are no longer another nervous candidate waiting to be selected. So, when you allow yourself to be that person, you will be. As my husband says to our son – "*Believe you and you will achieve*".

I often wonder, what makes someone a star, a team leader, a leader of a company or a nation? Apart from all the skills, talents et cetera necessary to perform the job. It is the one question I ask myself again and again. I have observed leaders and come to the conclusion that: *They allow themselves to be that person.* A great example of this is leaders who no one could think of as actually being leaders and yet they are the ones that are leading.

Very often, I speak to professionals where I can see clearly that they could take the next step and *own the crown* so to speak. Except there's this reservation within them, this self-judgment of: "What if I am not as good as I needed to be?" then, next comes the statement: "I am not ready". Even though they possess all of the necessary skills and qualifications and years of experience, they still tell themselves that they are not ready. When will we be ready? We can wait forever to be ready or we can simply tell ourselves; *the time is now! Just allow yourself to be ready and you are ready.*

The very first thing we do to 'ready' ourselves is to be steady and stand tall and embrace our own space, our own voice and our own presence. This is how we show that we believe in ourselves. It doesn't matter how others perceive us.

"Experience comes second but mind power comes first." – Linda Tomai Duong

This is a good time to remind yourself that there is no 'perfect' status. What is good or perfect for one person may not be good or near perfect for another. Opinions are just opinions and they are like a piece of artwork, in that, opinions are subjective and therefore we don't need to be 'good enough' for anybody else, but to think; *"I just need to give things a go and do my absolute best and be good enough for me"*.

Knowing that you have given things a go sincerely and have done your absolute best, with good, kind, and considerate intentions then, there is no guilt and no crime committed except to say or think to yourself that; *"This is me. This is my voice, my opinion, my best. You're welcome to accept it, take it or reject it and leave it. It is up to you."* When we take actions to do things. It is the intrinsic motivation which comes with contentment that we want and not the extrinsic motivation that often comes with pressure.

Intrinsic motivation refers to behavior that is driven by internal rewards such contentment, whereas, extrinsic motivation refers to behavior that is driven by external rewards such as money, fame, grades, and praise.

When we can believe in what we say, we own our own voice, our own space and stage. We have self-respect. That is self-belief and believing in ourselves. When we stay connected with ourselves so strongly, we will respond differently and more positively. Hence, we have a better chance at getting the job, and being the person that we are meant to be.

Mentors and Mentoring

Almost every successful person who has achieved great success will have had a mentor or two or even a few, whether it is in a paid or unpaid arrangement. Mentors can save us time and errors. Sharing insights and experiences that gives us perspective that we don't see on our own. A mentor who has been down the path that we want to travel can tell us the how, the what, the when, and the why it is better to do things a certain way, and it doesn't necessarily have to be one particular person only.

Formally speaking, mentoring is a collaborative engagement based on agreed expectations and goals between the mentor and the mentee. The aim is to assist the mentee with a positive learning experience, which can be mutually beneficial to both the mentor and mentee. It is a respectful relationship founded on the following: active and reflective listening, encouragement, constructive comments, openness, mutual trust, respect and a willingness to learn and share.

Over the years, I have been in both positions, and I had a number of mentors, mainly because I have many different interests. Also, because I love connecting with people wherever I go. I am aware of the teachers and mentors that exist around me all the time, and it doesn't have to be in a formal setting or formal arrangement. Sometimes, a child can be my mentor for that moment of time, depending on the circumstances. Being open-minded this way, gives me more access to learning.

I am a very enthusiastic person and a keen learner so I 'learn on the go' wherever I go. I feel that if you think that you are an expert, you will stop learning and you will lose out because the world continues to evolve daily. There are always new things happening. So I always consider myself the student, the newbie, the new kid on the block. This way I keep my mood upbeat and my curiosity high, and that makes my life journey more fun because I am always fresh and open-hearted. I am never old, regardless of my age.

Also, I grew up with the saying that, "A single conversation with a wise elder is worth many year's study of books". I learned this by being the seniors' audience when I was very young in Vietnam. I learn best in real life situations, and so I often like observing, and find mentors all the time in whatever I do, such as while attending networking functions, being out and making connections. Even in talking to children to understand how they think and feel from their age's point of view. Sometimes, I find a mentor even if it is just for the duration of an event. I always learn something new or am reminded of something I have forgotten.

Being a mentor can bring about a significant level of satisfaction and joy as well. In some cases, apart from contributing, it inspires you to achieve higher goals as you revisit your own skill sets and expertise in a specific area or you may end up, up-levelling your expertise while you are being a mentor. Especially when the focus is on the benefit of the mentee and not the pride of being a mentor only. It is a very rewarding way to share skills and knowledge, as well as a way to give back to the community. It also feels great to be able to contribute to other people's learning. One good way to form a mentor/mentee relationship is by volunteering at organisations or events.

If the relationship works out well, it can bring about great satisfaction and contentment, which leads to more happiness because the greatest feeling about being in the mentorship is the deep one-on-one connection. To connect with someone who has the same passion as you is the best kind of connection.

A mentor is like a walking cane to a blind person. A good mentor can pave the way and propel you to new heights that you may not have thought of before. A great mentor is paramount to success but it cannot happen without connection. So always reach out and connect.

While we discuss mentorship, it makes sense to cover the topic of learning because when we learn, we grow, and when we grow that is when we become more content.

Connection for Learning Success and Happiness

"Connecting the minds to the knowledge is the art of being a teacher."

— Linda Tomai Duong

For some people, learning new things is enough to bring them joy and happiness. Your mind gets the stimulation it craves, you get to meet new teachers, mentors, and friends. You get to connect in all areas; connecting your mind to the subject you are learning, connecting with the teachers and friends, which all brings about new hope, new ideas for creativity to grow, and it brings about the possibility of collaboration and for things to happen when opportunities are presented among friends.

In a normal classroom setting, there are three things that contribute to success in learning, apart from having the right teacher: They are; engagement, like-minded peers, and application. However, none of the above elements work if there is no connection. Connection to the teacher, connection to the peers, and connection to the subject itself. If you are a self-taught kind of learner, all you need is to feel the connection to the subject itself. If you do not feel the connection, learning cannot take place.

Let's say your company says every staff member needs to attend a first aid course. You will go but only because you have to. You may think "yeah, it's good to know. I'll go only because I have to." With this thought pattern and attitude for learning, you will learn but you won't get an A for your exam result. However, imagine, you are at the hospital, with your first newborn, and the doctor says: "Tomorrow, you're attending your first aid course and it's for your child's benefit that you learn this skill." Chances are you will make sure you arrive to class with a pen and a note pad and will give your undivided attention.

The point here is that you will become not only interested but fully engaged in learning when there is a connection to the purpose in learning. The meaning and the purpose for learning is the connection. This connection inspires you to undertake the learning whole-heartedly, and pushes you to achieve an A+ for your exam result. All teachers and educators know that engagement is the essential element for teaching and learning. Yet the secret to engagement and success in learning is *connection.*

This is why schooling in the infancy stages is all about play and fun because that's what children do; play and have fun. They don't think about learning at all. The children's connection to learning at this stage is play. Learning is an adult's agenda, and this is precisely why learning through play is so successful for the early years in education.

As the children grow older in the primary or elementary years, it is all about friendships and feeling included, as this is how the children feel the connection in learning and schooling; it is all about connecting with friends and what each other does. That is why schools and teachers place a lot of focus on ensuring the students feel included.

Towards later years in high school and college or university, it is all about self-identity, when students choose the subject field to major in for their studies. It is all about questioning; "Who am I?" and "What do I want to do in the world?" These are the questions that guide the individual's purpose and connect them in learning.

It could also be explained this way; for learning to happen, you need to be engaged in the learning process itself. If you cannot engage in the class, in the topic or in the discussions, that simply means you don't feel like you belong there in the class. This goes back to connection. Once you are connected with your peers, you will feel that you belong in the group. Then the learning process can take place and you can be actively interested in the learning. Otherwise, everything else seems to just occur outside of you; nothing is really interesting or exciting because you have disengaged yourself from the class altogether, making it difficult to achieve.

On the other hand, if you are enrolled in an interesting course with a very knowledgeable teacher and you have good connection with him or her, you will naturally participate, and you will also become more interested, driven and motivated by the teacher's suggestions and act on their feedback for improvement. Learning becomes more interesting and fun as you become more engaged, especially when like-minded peers stimulate each other as well; this can add even more enjoyment to the learning experience.

If you happen to have a teacher who you cannot connect with, you still can experience great learning by connecting to your like-minded peers. They will be the people that can help you stay engaged in learning. Often, it is your peers that will lift you to higher levels of achievement as you learn, inspire, support and challenge one another in the process.

When you are in an environment where everyone is interested, you will stimulate each other's learning and curiosity, and things become more fun. With good spirits, everyone contributes and lifts each other to a more successful learning journey. This applies to all levels from preschool and kindergarten through to university and work-related courses or training.

The other element that makes your learning journey a definite success is *application*. Some schools actually have an award for *Application and Attitude*. This is awarded to the students who have the right attitude to learning and *actually apply what they learn*. We all like to take notes when it comes to listening to lectures and learning. The important aspect for learning is - what you do with the notes is what matters.

Taking notes reinforces the lessons and helps us to remember what we have learned, which becomes knowledge. Knowledge alone does little for us. *Applying the knowledge is what gives us the results we desire.* It was once said that "knowledge is power". That was before the internet age. Now with the accessibility of the internet, knowledge itself is no longer the power; instead *application IS power.* Gaining knowledge is only useful if we can apply it and use it to make an impact. So, *Application is the main drive to success in learning.*

To aim for your achievements, it is good to begin with the 'end goal' in mind. This goes back to designing your own journey by looking down from the peak of the mountain, to get a clearer view so you can formulate your plan. Working backwards or examine the path by viewing it from the end of your goal will help you make the decision of whether a formal university is the path you need to take or some private commercialised courses are better. There are some confusing messages these days, with some successful entrepreneurs indicating that university is no longer the route to take, or no longer considered as important as it once was. In some fields, university is still the path to take. By looking at your end goal first, the path to take will be much clearer.

As the saying goes, *"when the student is ready, the teacher will appear"*. This, initially, has a literal meaning to me, as in when the student is ready; the teacher will physically appear, taking it as I will meet the right teacher. This is still true but more so, as time goes by, I realised that when we are *really* ready to learn, not only will we find the right teacher but *we will also be guided by ourselves, our own intuition, wisdom and our own higher-self within us*, with higher order thinking and deeper meaning, because we have been through the searching and seeking journey and are now ready to access the insightful information we have accumulated over the years. We then become our own teacher and guide.

Therefore, for learning to be successful, we must feel the connection to the learning environment, be it the teacher, the subject itself, and/or our peers in order to be engaged in what we learn and we must *apply what we learn* to see the benefits gained from our learning.

TIPS:

Quiet Leaders versus Loud Leaders

"True leaders don't tell people what to do – they inspire them into action!"

— Linda Tomai Duong

I learned from observing young children that leaders don't always have to be outspoken and have 'loud' personalities. They can be quiet leaders with their soft natured way of leading that can win more hearts and win far more effectively than the obvious prominent, dominant, louder leaders do. Because sometimes, the dominating kind of leaders operate from ego, whereas a quiet leader often leads out of care and concern. This is not an absolute and/or biased opinion but just what I have observed.

In sharing this, my purpose is to remind parents of quiet children who are concerned that their child may not get a chance at being a leader, to let go of those concerns; and to remind the loud leaders to be cautious of giving the wrong impression to others. It is amazing what we can learn from children if we pay attention to them.

As I continued to observe, I also realised that quiet leaders don't have competitors while loud, obvious leaders do. And, quiet leaders lead with more harmony. So if you're a quiet person by nature, don't under estimate your leadership powers.

"A leader is best when people barely know he exists; when his work is done, his aim fulfilled, they will say, we did it ourselves"

— Lao Tzu

"Are We There Yet?" versus "I am Never Going to Get There!"

It is fantastic to keep going upwards and onwards, provided we pause and enjoy the moments along the journey. It is much better to acknowledge what we have achieved and practicing gratitude for reaching our achievements rather than falling into the trap of being constantly struggling for further success; be mindful not to fall into the pattern where each time we have achieve our goals, we set the bar ever higher. While this is meant to stretch our abilities to bring out our best potential, sometimes it can do more harm than good. Because when we keep aiming for higher goals, we sometimes forget how far we have come, and instead of celebrating and being content, we dwell on the fact that we need to achieve more and so we become unhappy.

Reflecting on what has been achieved and appreciating our success is necessary, so that our 'chase' for the next goals or the next dreams does not make the previous one less valuable, or worse, puts us into an expectation, anxiety, and deflation mode. This is when we take away our own happiness without us realising it.

There is a misconception and worry that pausing will cause a loss of motivation to move forward and so we keep on going non-stop. This is what causes exhaustion and burnout. It is much better to have a balance where we can take breaks before we get to our health's breaking point, which takes us further away from our happiness that we have strived so hard to achieve. In fact, the opposite is true. When we do allow time to have an actual break, we can recharge, refresh, and regain our strength, and we will actually function more effectively.

The staff will take holidays, you too will take holidays, but can your mind take a holiday too? Your body may be on holidays but how about your mind? Is your mind really taking a break when you are on holidays?

The hype associated with the concept of working whenever you want, wherever you want, even when you travel is real; "You can work at any resort you choose around the world," which sounds all fancy and glamorous but, unfortunately, it has encouraged more attachment to the business than the longed for freedom. This has caused our minds to be busier and more overwhelmed than before this idea came about.

With the conventional way of working, at least there was a clear guideline as to your working hours and you knew that when you took a holiday, your mind was freed up for family, leisure and pleasure. The ability to access work constantly through technology can bring on more stress than freedom if we are not careful, which can also rob us of our precious happy moments. Whatever the end goal is, we will forever be chasing the next ones if we place the presence of happiness on external factors.

"When you offer services or products that fix a client's problems and pains, you are delivering a piece of calmness, joy, and happiness to the jigsaw of their ultimate happiness."

Linda Tomai Duong

"When you can see the bigger meaning of what you do and the end result that contributes to others' happiness, that is when you are serving your purpose in life."

Linda Tomai Duong

"When you lead a life that has deep connection to your work and live with passions, you are living your life on purpose."

Linda Tomai Duong

"The most valuable lessons are not those in school but in life — learning to connect with others."

Linda Tomai Duong

"Connecting the minds to the knowledge is the art of being a teacher."

Linda Tomai Duong

"Simply focus on connecting to the passion you have for the work you do, in and of itself. When you do that, it will give you the drive to come up with creative ways to do the job well."

Linda Tomai Duong

"Application is the main drive to success in learning."

Linda Tomai Duong

Chapter 9

Happiness in Finance through Business and Corporate Success

"Connection is the currency to business success."

— Linda Tomai Duong

When we think of business, we think of trading. Business is an exchange of goods and services for money. But let's not forget that there are humans involved. Humans, us, we, are the ones who run and drive the businesses. No connection means no business. Period.

Connecting with Emotional Intelligence for Business Success

Since businesses are run by humans, and humans crave connections, it really shows that no business or trading could be done if there are no connections made. Therefore, your level of success in connection equals your level of success in business dealings.

"Your level of success in connection equals your level of success in business dealings."

— Linda Tomai Duong

Even TV advertisements are not considered successful if they do not connect to their audiences, and the copywriters know what kind of customers they need to attract and those are the audiences they focus on connecting with, through their words during the entire advertisement being aired on TV.

When they communicate to these audiences, they already have the connection formula worked out. The colours, images, language, music and sounds, et cetera are chosen to ensure their advertisements are effective, including when and where they air it, at what time and on which channels. All these elements are planned to aim at the kind of people they want to connect to as their targeted audience.

It is all about connecting to the audiences' desires, wishes and needs. The invisible connections don't seem obvious to our eyes but they are felt through the emotions. The targeted audiences don't just see the products shown on the screen but also *feel and sense* the product and its benefits, such as perfumes and chocolates are the two quick examples which audiences can feel and sense the products' benefits as they view the advertisement being aired.

Connections are all about emotions and therefore *the application of connection is the use of the emotional intelligence* element in business dealings. Advertisements are effective only because they trigger the audiences' emotions, moving them into taking action.

Like the slogan *'Just Do It'* from a well-known shoe company, whose logo features a tick. Everything is designed to trigger emotions into action, and the audiences are connected to the feeling that has been evoked and hence being motivated into thinking that they are action takers if they buy those shoes.

"Without connection, TV advertisements would not be successful. No one would buy the services or products if no connections are made. Connection is the ultimate element of success for business."

— Linda Tomai Duong

Emotions are what drive our actions. That is what all the TV commercials use; connecting to the audiences' emotions and driving them to take action. This is how all the advertisements become so successful.

Another quick example is this, when the owner of a manufacturing company meets the owner of a distribution company to discuss collaboration and a business agreement; if no connections are made between them, (in another word, if they don't 'click' with each other), chances are the business talk will end very quickly. On the other hand, when they click and connect well, they are more than likely to do business with one another. So, if we create meaningful connections as we relate to each other in business dealings, rather than just focus on numbers, data and figures, we will do much better. *It is called using our emotional intelligence in business. To simplify this — **I call it using our authentic connections in business dealings and success.***

Applying Emotional Intelligence or Using Authentic Connections for Business Success

Emotional intelligence sounds like a complicated term, yet, to me it is all about feelings and connections. It is simply the application of connection with ourselves and with others, and being aware of our thoughts and emotions, and the ability to understand and manage your own emotions and the emotions of others, then use the emotional information to guide our thinking and behaviours, including using our intuitive feelings as well. This includes regulating your own emotions and cheering up or calming down other people, understanding your effects on others. This is particularly true when you are a manager or a leader of your team. It also includes emotional awareness; the ability to harness emotions, and apply them to tasks like thinking and problem solving.

The term Emotional Intelligence was formulated in 1990 in a research paper by two psychology professors, John D. Mayer of The University of New Hampshire (UNH) and Peter Salovey of Yale University. It took almost a decade later, for psychologist Daniel Goleman to establish the importance of emotional intelligence to business leadership. In 1998, in what has become one of *Harvard Business Review*'s (HBR) most enduring articles, *What Makes a Leader.*

In my situation, growing up with nine siblings spanning a 20-year age gap between the oldest and the youngest, and having 24 nieces and nephews, plus becoming an aunt at the age of five, you sure get to practice emotional intelligence, a lot. I'm talking about not only the pure practice but dealing with the challenges as well; as in how to use your emotional intelligence in such a way that it serves you as well as others, including the whole extended families belonging to your nine siblings. With so many different people involving multiple cultural differences from the brothers and sisters in-law, not to mention the extended in-law families, and the nieces and nephews that are born in Australia, as well as those are born overseas. It can be overwhelming at times. Yet, using my emotional intelligence from my home and family life has served me well in the business world. That is where your self-awareness, awareness of the clients, awareness of the employees, and awareness of the business or organisation as a whole come into play.

This is how I translated my family into my business model:

My parents: the CEOs of the company.

The older siblings: the directors and managers of the company.

Me: The PR/Mediator.

The younger sibling, nieces and nephews: staff, employees, peers.

The brothers-in-law, sisters-in-law , parents-in-laws: clients

Friends: support (just like the IT support team; if there is a glitch in the family, you go to your friends for support!).

What I am trying to share here is the different dynamics in relationships, and even though I *don't* consider my younger sibling, nieces and nephews as staff, and I *don't* consider my brothers-in-law, sisters-in-law and parents-in-law as clients. Still, you get the picture. There are levels and categories in relation to where you are and how you need to speak and relate to each group differently. It is exactly like how you would run a large company. It requires you tuning in and being aware of the dynamics and understanding each party's needs at different times.

Therefore, if we stay connected with our thought process, we will gain clarity and can focus better to achieve more. If we are more connected with our business in terms of being aware of clients' needs as well as employees' needs, we will form better visions and gain more team energy collectively, and can add more impact to increase the team's passion to drive those visions. When we stay connected with our clients, we can look after them better and will get more repeat business and referrals to help the business's growth. It is a very simple model for business success, yet applying connection and emotional intelligence to the business is crucial.

To be highly successful, there are three entities that we need to master in order to master a successful business or corporation, and they are; mastering our mind, mastering our core business and mastering our clients:

Mastering our mind: From my years of studying and working in different fields — whether it be Diversional Therapy, Primary teaching, Life Coaching and being a speaker and author, I've learned that one foundation element rings true — *success is all to do with our minds.* Dealing with the mind is an inner game. Our mind is the first thing we need to master, in order to determine what our results and outcome will be. Self-belief is a must-have element in order to succeed.

"Whether you think you can or whether you think you can't, you're right," said Henry Ford, proving that self-confidence is an absolute must have for success to come. It is an 'inner game'.

"Master your mind and you master your life, including your business."

— Linda Tomai Duong

Mastering our core business: Applying emotional intelligence to all areas of your business means building a business based on care and concerns, rather than basing it on only numbers and figures. Care and concerns are the emotions that provide the driving force for us to see the bigger vision and mission in what we do. Therefore, we need to focus more on human connections, rather than just focusing on data and reports.

Emotions are what help drive actions and help you to connect with your team members more, so that they can feel and see your mission and vision, to help bring it to life. People are what drives a business. It makes sense to connect with each other more and care more for your team, so that they can share your drive and be inspired to reach for the same common goals. As the saying goes: "Together, we achieve more".

Mastering our clients: We all want to feel that others care about us, to feel important and feel valued. Clients of any business desire the same feeling, which is to be cared for and valued. Investing in showing the clients how much they are valued is better than investing in advertising to attract new clients if you had to choose between the two methods of client retention.

One of the most direct ways to show your clients that they are valued is to connect with them, and make them feel important, such as offering free birthday meals if you run a restaurant or a free hair blow-dry if you operate a hair salon, for example. Gestures like this will help you to build loyal and long-term clients, because when they are happy, they will refer more clients and word-of-mouth referrals are the best form of advertising.

The Evolution of Connection

Minimal Connection: In the past, most work was done in a factory and people worked with machinery and conveyor belts. This meant that each person was in charge of a 'station' along the mass production assembly line and there were minimal opportunities for close human interaction throughout the day.

Realising Connection is Important: Fast forward to the 1980s and 1990s, this was the time when people really sang *"It's not what you know, it's who you know..."* The trend was that if you decided where you wanted to be in terms of career and financial success, you connected with smart people, to look well, to look rich, it also meant you would associate with people who played golf at a country club, for example, so that you would get to rub shoulders with the rich and famous.

People wanted to connect with others for specific reasons, with specific end goals in mind, for their own benefit. As a result, although they may have succeeded financially or business wise, at the end of the day or at the end of that journey, they were still not completely happy, not feeling completely satisfied or feeling fulfilled. They still felt like something was missing. Their happiness was missing because the focus of the connection was outcome driven and often began with the end purpose in mind. This is not meant to be a judgmental note but simply an observation.

Realising Connection is a Must in the Business World: Friendship and genuine connection was the missing element to feel fulfilled in business dealing. By 'friendship' I do not mean that we have to be friends with every single person we have a business dealing with. However, if we apply the concept of friends to the business world, it does mean that the customer is my friend and I am going to look after the customer's best interests to the best of my ability. Hence, the sales guy is not seen as just 'the sales guy!' but as a person who brings joy from the product he sells. This way, the concept of friendship in business relationships has a 'two-way thought processes' where the focus is mutual respect for mutual benefits to create win/win situations.

This way you will be dealing in business in an honest, caring and authentic manner. Selling products that only bring more benefits and joy to your customers. This approach means that we do works that serve with consciousness that brings about happiness to ourselves and to others. This is when we will realise what our life purpose is.

It only makes sense for us to see and create win-win situations in business dealings when we see each other's visions and missions.

"When authentic connections happen, friendships grow, whether it is in a personal setting or in the business world. Friendship is what makes interactions and connections feel complete and brings about happiness."

— Linda Tomai Duong

There are three things that ensure a business has longstanding and loyal customers; *honesty in business dealings, respect* for customers and *integrity in our dealings.*

If we were all to run businesses and treat clients based on the 'two-way street', like a friendship model, where we care about each other, then there would be no fraud. Every business that treats its customers well will most definitely get more referrals and repeat customers. This not only builds a strong client base for the stability and sustainability of the business but also makes our jobs a lot more meaningful, and we in turn receive more joy at work than just receiving monetary payment.

Do you remember how it feels when you receive testimonials, flowers, chocolates, photos and heartfelt thank you letters from clients who show how much they really appreciate what you do and your services? This does not only apply to individual business and client relationships but also within an organisation between employees and owners of an organisation and vice versa.

Many people have achieved great business and financial success but they miss the authentic connections. We need emotions and connections to nurture our soul on a daily basis, otherwise we will get deflated and eventually burn out.

This doesn't mean we have to share all our personal details but it is about being genuine in connecting, treating each other with respect, honesty and integrity, keeping the communication lines open, maintaining both parties' interests in mind. If we do this, we all will feel more fulfilled and be happier at work, and in our business.

Connection for the Entrepreneurs and Solo-preneurs

Many entrepreneurs, especially solo-preneurs know how lonely and isolated it can be when we are all busy doing our own thing and many end up experiencing burn out, isolation and depression.

However, once we start connecting, we can support each other a lot better. We can use each other's services and give referrals to help build one another's business. Hence, more and more networking clubs and events are becoming increasingly successful. As we connect with each other, we need to remember that *it is not what we sell but how we sell* that is important. It all comes down to how we connect with each other.

There are three areas that can help solo-preneurs succeed:

Connecting With Clients Increases Sales: When making a sales call or giving a sales presentation, be mindful to aim for authentic connections rather than just the end result. Be present and connect sincerely to enjoy the process rather than only aiming for the sale only. Evoking positive feelings and emotions is what helps a client to decide whether or not they will buy from you or work with you.

Have you ever gone window shopping, not planning to buy but the sales lady is so welcoming that you end up buying something because her warm greeting has made you feel good?

From the first moment of your name being heard to the minute you get to present your work, whether you realise it or not, you are connecting with your potential and future customers, clients, and audiences. Keep in mind that when you are talking to a potential client and if they are undecided, they are listening, liking what you say but they have not yet decided to buy your product or service. Instead of losing patience and feeling frustrated that you cannot close the sale and wanting to rush off the phone, be patient and allow a bit more time and keep connecting and aim for future sales and referrals instead of the immediate sale only. Apart from that, if you enjoy our job, it will only add more joy to have the opportunity to share about what you do. Sharing and connecting equals happiness. So, that's the alternate win if you have experienced joy out of the connection time.

Time is precious and it will be wasted if you rush off without a sale, *and/or* future referral potentials, and both parties go away feeling disappointed. Yet, it will still be worthwhile to continue connecting and do your best to maintain the connection, because even if the client doesn't buy this time, they may still refer you on to others if they enjoy your connection after all, and the is happiness for you both while connecting. Also, never underestimate the power of word-of-mouth referrals. It is the best form of advertising, when you have fans raving about you and your services, and it is free. Ultimately, when we connect sincerely, both parties can experience joy from the act of connection itself.

When I had my bridal boutique, most of the new clients were referred to me by either previous clients, or people who had walked or driven past the boutique and liked the look of it. I had the local Chambers of Commerce sent out mystery shoppers to test me on my customer's services quality and I had no idea when it happened but suddenly I was invited to attend the award event as I was one of the award receivers. I also had one groomsman visit with the bridal group and say: "So, you're Linda! And this is Snow White Bridals! I've heard all about you in every gathering, every dinner for the past months!" This is not to boast about my achievements but to share the importance of never underestimate the power of referrals. That is connection with clients at its best, plus a raving fan.

Connecting with Yourself Results in More Time in a Day: Do you wish you have more time in day? We all do. Being a solopreneur is highly challenging as you wear many hats. Before you know it, you sit in the prison of your own long to-do list and stress. Which contradicts with the reasons why you wanted to run your own business, to be your own boss to begin with, and to have more time to do what you want to do. However, now, suddenly you are trapped with all the to-dos. In order to have more time and gain back your freedom, you need to check in and connect with yourself more often.

You need to check in with the following questions:

Will I enjoy this project?

Will I learn new things and grow personally from this project?

Will it help grow my business instead of just bringing in more money?

Will this project serve others as well?

Is it going to be enjoyable and add more fun in my life?

Does working on this project contribute to the lifestyle I want to create or keep me so busy that it will take me away from the lifestyle I desire? (Remember, this was probably the reason why you wanted to run your own business in the first place, to have the freedom of choice in choosing the work you want to do).

Will this project help I choose the clients I want to work with?

Will I be able to make decisions based on what brings me joy rather than just how much money it brings in?

Will the business deal make my life better and not just bring in more money?

Will it bring me more credibility and fame? If so, what does it mean to me? (As not everybody wants fame).

Sometimes, it is a challenge for this decision-making process. However, do remember, that the happy feeling of achieving financial success or social status does not last forever as business success fluctuates. It is the contentment and fulfillment in running a business that got you to work for yourself.

Lastly, the most crucial question is; what is your currency? Is it money, fame, time, or happiness? What do you work for? Remember to keep this in mind when making business decisions.

Some people don't mind to do volunteering work because what they get paid in the end is the satisfaction from contributing to others. Their currency is happiness from within.

Networking — Connection with Industry Peers: When customers deal with a solo-preneur, it's often the person that comes to mind before their products or services do. So the emphasis has to be on the importance of being authentic, sincere and caring while you offer your products and services, because they represent you. So it is not always who you can sell to or what you have to offer them. But instead, think of who you can refer to each of those businesses as well. That way the whole circle of networkers gets to become a strong connection hub for each other. Always think of the two-way street model and there will be continuous beneficial connections.

"Authentic connection equals business success."

— Linda Tomai Duong

The Connection Hubs

I can see a future where we have large business hubs where solo-preneurs can connect more with each other instead of being isolated in their own little office or at home. They can network and refer clients to each other more frequently.

Each hub has café bars where each solo-preneur or business can hire a lounge booth as their office, a place to see clients. Waiters and waitresses will serve breakfast, lunch, dinner and coffee throughout the day. This way we can all look after each other and have more connections and keep each other happy.

We all know that being an entrepreneur and a solo-preneur is hard. You do everything on your own and there is only one pair of hands and only so many hours in a day, and so sometimes we skip meals, start to get tired, become unwell and eventually burn out.

No health equals no wealth.

Health must be the first priority in achieving financial success. However, if there is no connections, it will affect our mental health. That is why we need to be mindful that happiness and fitness go hand-in-hand together, which we will also discuss in the following chapter as one of the elements in achieving happiness.

With these Connection Hubs, my concept is that the entrepreneurs and solo-preneurs get to be looked after by the café staff with good quality food. The café owners get more regular patrons. The clients that come for business meetings, or for the services such as consulting, coaching, group meetings, networking, or any similar kind of work also gain the benefits of being served and looked after by the café staff. They may even find work there as they make connections. These Connection Hubs would be a great central place for business as well as social connections to occur.

Of course, each hub would include a central place for printers and all other office needs, rooms for meetings, seminars and networking events, for all of the businesses to use. I would love to see this happen. So if you decide to start one, be sure to contact me. I envision that we will see Connection Hubs happening around the world.

Such hubs serve multi-purposes including: Connections for all, on-the-spot referrals of networks for businesses as well as employment, and the added convenience of having meals and a café service that caters to all.

"Connection is the currency to success and happiness in business."

— Linda Tomai Duong

Connecting with Emotional Intelligence for Corporate Success

The benefits of connection work the same way for any organisation or corporation. In general, people leave their jobs because either their skills have outgrown their job, they don't see opportunities for promotion or growth, or they are offered better incentives and higher pay elsewhere and, last but not least, they don't like their boss. For all the earlier listed reasons, we can still drag on, ponder, and tolerate, but not the last reason. Unless someone is really desperate to keep their job in order to make a living. Everyone knows it can be almost impossible to stay on in a job when you don't like your boss*.

*Please see tips at the end of this chapter for ideas on how to deal with this situation.

When we work at the same job day in, day out, it can become tedious after many years, and if you don't get along with your boss as well, then, that is depleting, frustrating and unsatisfying — all the opposite feelings that contribute to happiness. In fact, this one reason alone is the most crucial one in driving someone to actually take action and leave.

However, in organisations where the leaders create an environment that nurtures a culture of connectedness and positive connections, such organisations will have happier employees, as they often treat each other with a 'we are a happy family model'. They will fight for their team and stand up for each other, and back each other up when needed. In such a working culture, employees feel that they belong and can connect with each other well. As a result, joy and happiness in the workplace are increased, which minimises the likelihood of employee resignations, in turn saving organisations a lot of expenses from staff turnover.

Authentic connection is what humans yearn for; the connection from human to human is what makes our days exciting, fun, or emotional, and supportive connections add meaning to the job and make it not just another business encounter, not just another job, day in, day out, that drains us.

Each time we connect, we can ignite each other's emotions and that is when we are driven to take action. This is when we feel alive and can stay at the same job for many years, because it is not just the job itself that keeps us there but also the people we work with that make all the difference.

I can understand that for some of us who have family and are busy, we can't wait until the end of the day to go home and see our loved ones. But there are others that may have lost their loved ones, be it through sickness, terrorism, war, natural disasters, or separation and divorce. Et cetera. Work could be the only place they can connect with others, to hear their own voice before they go back to their isolation, and their own loneliness at home. All they need is to have someone to listen sincerely to them even just for a few minutes to feel 'alive' and to feel the empathy that all human needs. The empathy mentioned here, does not have to be long talks as we are at work but it is the basic humanly kind of empathy to remind us that; there are others here, and that we are not alone. It could simply be a sincerely comment of sharing what you had for dinner last night, or what you do in the weekend? A sincere conversation is what brings about connection between two people. Sometimes, by simply listening, we can lift others pains. This is not meant to add more onto already busy life but to simply be mindful of this fact and extend our compassion at work whenever we can while earning money, as it would help bring happiness to others in the simplest, yet profound way.

It is people that make it fun, and/or meaningful. Being able to connect with others makes us feel more alive! We feel more alert when we get to connect openly and deeply to others at work; it enhances our enjoyment and job satisfaction, which can inspire us to commit to a job for a longer period of time.

Moreover, with good connections, employees are more motivated to go to work, resulting in a decrease in sick leave, and an increase in productivity and profits. They will also be more in line with the organisation's vision and mission as they are connected more with the leaders. The organisation also benefits from better cooperation between the staff members, which builds stronger team work, as all team members are moving towards the organisation's goals in synchronisation and harmony.

When the leader shares her goal with the team and has the team's support, together they can achieve the goal far better when they stay connected as a team, and when you have team unity, it breaks down team barriers, that way, you can have more collaboration to focus on the same goal. Teams that have strong connections win far more frequently than those that have fewer connections with each other within the team.

Connection and winning not only promotes an uplifting spirit at work and lifts morale, but also increases joy at work, which contributes greatly to the betterment of employees' health as well as benefiting business owners and organisations. Strong connections and employee wellbeing can also save a company from the expense of employees taking frequent sick leave. In summary: ***Connection means health and wealth of a company, business and staff.***

While team leaders are the ones to lead, employees can make a difference too, in terms of creating a more positive work environment and building more connections. As an individual, we can certainly take the initiative to connect with our colleagues, team leaders and management personnel. We all can take the initiative to connect with others and inspire each other in our own way. For example, the team leader or CEO may be great at what they do at work but they are still human and crave connection. You can break the barrier by sharing a little about yourself, such as what you cooked for dinner, or talk about a new book you've read or share when you've found a new interesting café. Any small talk is a great start to make connections.

Sometimes, when we keep to ourselves, it can project a misconception, and people start to formulate all sorts of views on us and vice versa. We just never know, it could be that s/he has just gone through a divorce and needs some connection time to help ease the pain. Or s/he is actually an orphan who has lost all of his/her family to terrorism or some natural disaster. You never know... A little compassion goes a l o n g w a y.

Once we open up and invite conversations, we can be surprised at what each other does or how much we can inspire one another. Understandably, those with busy family commitments may not have the time and energy to do more than their job. However, simply by being open and connecting authentically whenever you can is all you need to do, to help build a warm, connected work environment for yourself and others.

In order to bring more happiness into the business world, we need to connect with each other more authentically. People tend to want to know who makes up the team, and who is behind the company name, what they think and believe and what their vision and mission are.

More and more businesses have realised by now that we need to have not only the customers' interests in mind but also the employees' benefits and wellbeing at the forefront of their daily business — without the employees, there will be no staff to provide goods and services. Business is no longer operating for the purpose of making money and profit only. If we want to create a better world for the future, we must be aware of the need to operate with a social consciousness in mind. When we do this, it is a win-win situation for all.

"Authentic connection is what humans yearn for. Human to human, authentic connections that have meaning and not just business dealings."

— Linda Tomai Duong

TIPS:

If we want to be a visionary, we need to realise that it involves others and the universe at large. We must accept that we cannot do it alone. To create a future or advancements in a creative and imaginative way, we need team work, and *connection is the key element of team work.*

A visionary is someone that thinks about the future or advancements in a creative and imaginative way. Visionaries are usually ahead of their time and have a powerful plan to bring about positive change in the future. They need to build a team to carry out the mission, and so connection is an absolutely vital element for success for a visionary, and their work ultimately brings about happiness for all.

Tip 1

The following are four basic but effective team building exercises that can be implemented easily:

Exercise A - Sharing is connecting

Time: 1 — 2 minutes

Number of Participants: Two or more people

How to play: Before a meeting, have every attendee walk around and share one-on-one what they hope to contribute to the meeting (based on the agenda) with as many people as possible.

If you want, offer a prize for the person who shares with the most number of people, and another prize for the person whose contributed idea received the most votes.

For example: The agenda is – How to promote more connection at work

The idea could be: Each person shares what they cooked or had for dinner the night before.

Objective: Improves meeting productivity and makes attendees engage and think about how they're going to contribute, rather than just what they hope to get out of the meeting.

Exercise B - Turn Negatives into Positives

Time: 5-6 minutes

Number of Participants: Two or more people

How to play: Partner a shares something negative that happened in their life with Partner B. It can be a personal or work-related, but it has to be true. Then Partner A discusses the same experience again, but focuses only on the positive points. Partner B helps explore the hopeful side of the bad experience. Afterwards, they switch roles.

Objective: Participants discover how to reframe negative situations into learning experiences together. This is to remind the staff about bring a positive mind frame to work and life.

Exercise C - Creating loyalty club meet ups

This is great for many types of business. This not only creates a hub for like-minded people to connect but also builds a connecting community over time, which essentially can help prevent isolation and depression in solo-preneurs and individuals. Also if you have found others to have the same mission as you, a collective voice is stronger than a single voice.

Tip 2

When a boss is not a nice boss.

You have two choices:

Leave or stay.

Leaving is easier but there's no guarantee that you won't run in another unpleasant boss.

By staying you also have a few choices:

Leave things the way they are but then of course you would still be unhappy at work.

Find peace in yourself. Easier said than done. But possible.

You/we all have the power to inspire change. Allow truckloads of patience and attention, you will find ways that you can inspire him/her in your own way. From the smallest action such as smile more, stay positive regardless of their poor behavior, keeping things on a professional level, et cetera. It takes effort but the result is very empowering and satisfying if you can inspire the change for the better in your boss.

"Authentic connection is what we yearn for. Human to human, connections that have meaning and not just another business dealings."

Linda Tomai Duong

"Connection means health,
and equals wealth."

Linda Tomai Duong

"Connection is the currency to business success and happiness in business."

Linda Tomai Duong

"Your level of success in connection, equals your level of success in business dealings."

Linda Tomai Duong

"The most valuable lessons are not only those in school but in life — learning to connect
with others."

Linda Tomai Duong

"Connection means health, and wealth of a company."

Linda Tomai Duong

"Connection is the currency to success and happiness in business."

Linda Tomai Duong

Chapter 10

Happiness in Fitness

"We need a healthy body to house a healthy mind!"

— Linda Tomai Duong

Health Equals Wealth

Health is the fourth of the five elements that help us to stay connected. Our health connects to everything we do. We take our health for granted, when we need to guard it and look after it as the highest priority on our to-do list. We also expect that we can walk, talk and run as if they are our birth-right. Sadly, not everyone has all of these basic yet essential and precious motor abilities.

I have no sickness and, as healthy as I am at present, but I have experienced losing some of the most basic human abilities at different times, such as talking, walking and running. It was nothing drastic and yet it was enough to make me realise how much we take the ability to walk and talk for granted.

When I was 16 years old, I had a bad tooth that needed to be removed. Picture this; me, very petite (I weighed about 35kg at the time) and the dentist, tall and big in size with a pair of giant hands. The tooth was the second last one, and he was trying to reach in but his huge hand covered his view of the inside of my mouth. What did he do? He pressed my jaw to open it wider and CLICK it went!

I woke up the next day in pain because he had broken my jaw. I had to hold my jaw to talk and could only eat mashed food for the next two months. That was when I realised I actually love talking! This love of talking was also emphasised when I lost my voice a couple of months later, when I had laryngitis. I tried to talk but no voice came out. For a few days I had to communicate by writing, and it was frustrating to have to write a conversation, which takes much longer time then when you can say it in seconds.

The preciousness of health was further demonstrated and emphasised to me when I was pregnant with my first child. It was a rather extreme and difficult case of pregnancy. I could only walk on one foot, and tip- toed on the other from the twenty-seventh week of my pregnancy onwards. I had to limp to get to places with my big belly. Limping in pain with a big belly was no fun. That was when I realised how free and easy it is to be able to just walk and get to places with two legs. Such simple thing in life that we take for granted.

I was restricted by how far I could walk. My doctor recommended a walking frame but I refused it. Thinking back, I should have accepted the walking frame… The worst thing was I had to sit in a reclining position even to eat and my belly was my dining table. When I dropped things on the floor, I couldn't just bend down and pick it back up. I also couldn't sit up and had to have bed rest or sit reclining most of the time, which in the end caused a lot of back pain from the awkward siting position.

My health situation was not the worst compare some others' situations, but it was enough to illustrate to me how precious health is. It was enough for me to appreciate how good it is to be able to have the basic mobility and a physical voice. So, in sharing this, I am hoping to remind you with a message to look after your health and take action before it is too late!

Health and Achievement

"Health is our most precious wealth!"

– Linda Tomai Duong

The more you achieve, the more you need your health because the more we want to achieve, the more demand is put on our bodies. We all know this and yet we forget or ignore it. We let our life's *busYness* get in the way and we leave our exercise regime last on the to-do list. We keep saying we have no time to exercise until the day comes when we have no choice but only time for sickness. In order to keep on achieving, we need to maintain our optimal health.

Balance is the key.

Maintaining a balanced life routine is super crucial as it affects your families too.

Good health is something you can easily take control of, simply by attending to it early on. *Prevention is the cure when it comes to health and fitness*, otherwise we will see happiness being replaced with frustration and resentment as fitness restrictions and health scares set in.

If you don't have the health you want, life is not fun. If you cannot go skiing with your children because you have a bad back due to poor posture from long days spent sitting at work, then that's when you miss out on the fun and your happiness with your family, which is an integral part of the happiness in your life.

Many people find it best to do the exercise of their choice; whether it is walking, running or swimming, for example — in the morning before the work day starts so that it is done and out of the way before the day's busy schedule sets in. Others prefer to exercise at the end of the day. Planning and scheduling time for your exercise helps keep it a routine, otherwise it is very easy to skip, which results us in poor health or poor fitness levels.

Also, remember to ease your stiffened muscles and stimulate your blood circulation. If sit for a long time, make sure you get up regularly take short walking breaks to the tea break room to replenish with regular refill of water. Sometimes we become so focus in what we do that we forget to drink water. This is not to be used as unproductive time at work but to sincerely take care of yourself so that you can minimise sick leave. Also, by simply wriggling your toes and flexing your feet to stretch your calves while sitting at work can help too if you sit a lot like I do when writing. I am aware of the new disease — 'Death by Sitting' so I do what I can to keep my blood circulation moving. I also find that doing sit ups during my breaks can be quite effective, quick, and easy. If you are less physical and enjoy gentle exercise, there are many exercises that can be done lying down if you need to avoid rigorous exercise. Just do what works best for you. But do something.

Apart from physical exercise, it is important to have down time and relaxation time to rejuvenate and avoid burn outs. Do yoga or have massage. Watch a movie to unwind and relax your mind; please note here that it is to relax your mind, so comedy movies would be much better than scary movie as that stimulates and causes more stimulations and stress to the mind.

Taking some time out is the most basic, easiest way to avoid the build-up of stress and depression. Getting out in the sun for a few minutes a day is the quickest and simplest way to recharge is with the energy from the sun. You just need to get outside and stand in the sun for a few minutes a day, it helps us to connect to our environment while getting some fresh air as well as vitamin D. Very simple, easy but effective.

If you ever feel that you are running low on energy, just pause and refill by being outdoor, connecting with nature, animals, on your own or with others will help. I know this sounds super simple and logical but not everyone does it. Some people keep on going and keep ignoring the signals and symptoms until they can ignore them no more. To use a car as a metaphor: you cannot keep on driving unless you refill the petrol tank. Without our health, we cannot generate wealth. If we are sick, we simply can't work and present our optimal performance.

Your Mind is Your Power

We all know that a truly healthy person is not just physically healthy but more so mentally healthy. Health is inevitably a body and mind combination and is inseparable. There are more and more people experiencing mental health issues these days. Therefore, apart from the external parts of our body, we also need to look after our mind. The most amazing power is our mind power.

One little fun exercise that I do with my children is I will say: "OK, power mind time. We want to have a parking spot right in front of McDonald's OK? Because we are in a hurry today." Then we all focus on that one single thought, and guess what? We get a parking spot where we want, each and every time.

Basically, all it is, is that we become very focused on the task at hand, and we see things more precisely and focus more intently than we would at other times, and so we can achieve what we aim for. However, we can only do this if our minds are in a clear and calm state, and not overcrowded. This is why we need to practice mindfulness exercises to clear our minds often.

We hear of mindfulness often and at times it is often associated with deep spiritual talks that can shy people away. So let's have a look at what it is all about and how it can enhance our happiness.

According to the *Oxford Dictionary*:

Mindfulness is a mental state achieved by focusing one's awareness on the present moment, while calmly acknowledging and accepting one's feelings, thoughts and bodily sensations.

To me, basically, it simply means to be aware of the thoughts you have going in and hear the response of your inner thoughts as well during those moments, at the same time understanding how you feel.

Simply put, mindfulness is 'Catching' our thoughts, especially when negative thoughts surface, we can chose to attend to it, process it or let it pass. Tune in with the thought process. It is about being attentive to gain clarity and to clear away any stressful or distracting thoughts to maintain the balance in the mind and ultimately retain our peaceful state.

When we are being mindful of our thoughts, we will naturally think with more positive thought patterns, which helps to build a healthy mind and body, and naturally resulting us feeling happier when we are in good health.

Take a Conscious Breath

I strongly believe that there is **ONE** simple and **FREE** health tool that we can all access at anytime, anywhere. However, not everyone makes use of it. *It has invisible power to heal us and give us strength at any given time in any given situation — it is a Big Deep Breath.*

Taking *conscious breaths*, as I call it, can calm our nerves and increase our balance for wellbeing. Some breath control techniques found in yoga and meditation can help to manage stress and depression-related conditions.

I have been inspired by cases of stage four cancer patients whom were initially advised to get ready to say goodbye forever to their loved ones, yet they have been saved through the practice of yoga. These cases were in a documented film.

Another mindful related therapy approach that has really inspired me is Mindfulness-integrated Cognitive Behaviour Therapy. It offers a practical set of evidence-based techniques derived from mindfulness training together with the principles of Cognitive Behaviour Therapy (CBT) to address a broad range of psychological disorders and general stress-related conditions.

The formal term for doing *conscious breathing* is mindfulness done during meditation exercises. Many people find the term mindfulness and meditation old-fashioned and boring, and so I have given it a new name — *Conscious Breathing*, because to me, it is all about being aware of your breathing, and consciously taking the much needed breaths, hence I gave it that name so that it is easier to relate to and simpler to do.

As old-fashioned as it is, conscious breathing or meditation is an absolutely essential activity for long-term health. Meditation has been around for thousands of years and *it is boring because that is the purpose.* The whole purpose is to limit the stimulations to the minds so that we can slow down and achieve calmness, in our day-to-day lives. The more we do and achieve, the busier our mind becomes and it gets overcrowded with information, thoughts and decisions, and can cause stress. Meditation will help us clear the mind, destress, and allow us to achieve higher visions. Without a clear vision, we cannot achieve our ultimate dreams.

At times, you will find that by taking a big deep breath, it can even determine the outcome of your actions. Especially when faced with challenges, a big deep breath can give you the power to leap forward. Without it, you might retreat and lose that opportunity. Therefore, being a loser or winner can very much be depended on taking just one big deep breath.

In dealing with conflicts and difficult situations, it makes a huge difference between reacting and responding; just one big breath is all you need to give you the calmness you need, to respond instead of to react. In some extreme cases, it can even mean a life or death outcome, such as to jump out of the aero plane for a chance of survival, or stay in the aero plane and accept your 'predetermined' destiny.

The most basic way to make mindful breathing a new habit, is to think of it as doing conscious breathing. When it is put this simply, all you have to do is become 'conscious' of your breathing. Make sure you breathe deeper, slower and more regularly. This is not anything new but a great reminder for us all to remember to actually practice it – do slow breathing throughout the day.

It is easy to do and easy to add into your daily routine. Every morning as you get up and every night before you lay your head down, do this; close your eyes so that you can focus on your breathing, straighten your arms out, with your palms facing up, breathe in and out deeply and slowly, paying attention to your breath, the sensation through your nostrils and feel your chest rise and fall. Do it three times, which means only three breaths to begin with. Then slowly add more as you wish. It is the simplest way to start calming down an over active mind, quieten down any doubtful voices, and to clear any overcrowded thoughts.

You can do this while sitting by the edge of your bed or standing up. It really is the simplest way to start a mindfulness exercise. It might feel unnatural at first but once you start and do it sincerely, you will feel the benefit of even just taking three conscious breaths. Before you know it, it will be a new habit that you love, and soon you will want to do it longer and look for ways to do more breathing exercises or meditation. It really helps to clear your mind and to help you stay centred and focused to begin your day, and most importantly, to see your vision and mission in life clearer and sooner.

While running or walking in the park, remember to pause and enjoy the flowers. Listen to the birds. Look at the puppies having fun fetching their balls and bones. If your mind is full of worrying thoughts, anxiety or sadness, excitement or overwhelm, just park them ALL aside for a moment and you will feel lighter. You can always resume those thoughts later. By just parking them momentarily, set them aside, you will remember to feel the breeze, appreciate the bird or dog you see, and at the end you will feel lighter and clearer in your mind.

It is really that simple – be outside, park the thoughts, enjoy the air, and you will feel lighter.

Any time I feel sad or worry, I go out to the sun and this simple thought of appreciating that the sun gives life and that without the sun there would be no life – was enough a reminder to bring me back to the thought of how precious things are in life. When you have a deep appreciation for such simple thing, you will discover a kind of deeper joy and inner peace that you have not noticed before. This kind of joy and happiness is so simple yet so deep at the same time. It's so pure, and so easy for you to access, if you allow it.

Happiness is here and it is already inside you. Seek no more and just feel it. You can access happiness right here, right now. Feel the warmth of the sun. Hear the birds chirping. See the dog running in the park with and the beautiful flowers and trees.

B r e a t h e s l o w l y and deeply.

Pause.

Count to 10 if you need to but simply let go of all the busy thoughts, relax, and appreciate what's in front of you and enjoy the appreciative feeling.

You will feel the lightness afterwards and sense the joy and peace that you have ignited.

You are with happiness, and happiness is with you.

TIPS FOR FUN:

Just for fun, for a laugh, for good health, and for a quick boost and to lift your mood or give your active mind a break from its daily routine and stress, get your body moving and try any of the following activities:

Aerobics, Acrobatics, Abseiling, Archery

Badminton, Basketball, Belly dancing

Chinese Handball, Canoeing, Cartwheeling

Dancing of any kind, Darts, Dragon Boat Racing

Echoing, Equestrian

Fishing, Football

Gardening, Golfing

Handball, Horse riding

Ice Hockey, Ice-skating

Jogging, Jumping ropes

Karate, Kendo, Kick boxing,

Laughing, Laughing exercises

Lawn Bowls, Laser tag, Line dancing

Massage, Mountain Biking

Netball, Nine Pin Bowling, Nordic Skiing

Painting, Pool (Pocket Billiards), Puppy chasing, Pilates

Quacking (good for vocal exercise, Quid ditch (Muggle Quid ditch)

Rolling on the grass, Rope Climbing, Roller Skating

Swimming, Sailing, Surfing, Snow Skiing

Tennis, Table Tennis, Taekwondo

Uno cards, Under-water photography

Volleyball, Vault

X-boxing, Xylophone practice

Walking, Water Polo, Water Skiing

Yo-yo, Yak Polo, Yodelling, Yoga

Zig Zag walking, Zorb Football, Zumba

The above listed exercise is not all practical, but is again to trigger you thinking out your routine thoughts. Everything begins with our thoughts. Everything action is motivated by emotions and here, the emotion to elicit is fun. If you think of exercise is a chore and hard-work, you are unlikely to do it but if you think of exercise is fun, chances are you will be more encouraged to do it. We all like to have fun, so whatever you do, associate fun with it and you will feel lighter, easier, and most importantly you will feel more motivated to do it.

Once you get active and do fun activities, it is easier and more natural to have a positive outlook on life. Once you are positive, your health is better, and vice versa, when your health is good, you naturally are more positive. Health and positivity are interconnected and inseparable.

We also need to remind ourselves to be positive even when life throws adversity at us, as those are the times when we tend to forget about being positive easily, and remember to make use of the free tool of taking *conscious breaths* as often as needed. It helps you to be more relaxed, to achieve a more positive mind-frame, which in turn brings about optimum health.

Another fun thing to do is to tell jokes. It is said that "Laughter is the best medicine". Laughter is a healing tool without expense. It relaxes the mind and body, relieves physical tension and stress. It can chase away anxiety and depression, and even boosts the immune system. It also makes your heart feel lighter. Good health and hearty laughter are the cure for all types of diseases. So keep on doing deep breathing and laughing, it will make your heart feel more content; it will bring you joy and happiness. The effort invested in good health is definitely worthwhile because I am sure you would agree that; *"happiness is another form of wealth!" – Linda Tomai Duong.*

However to me personally – "happiness is the most treasured form of wealth!" – Linda Tomai Duong.

**"A Big Deep Breath
can help you leap!
A Laugh can cure
a Frown…**

**Both have invisible powers
to help avoid a mental
breakdown."**

Linda Tomai Duong

Chapter 11

Happiness in Fidelity

Self-Love => Love for Life => Greater Love = Compassion

"We gain deeper happiness and true contentment when we bring happiness to others."

— Linda Tomai Duong

This last element of the five foundation elements to happiness is fidelity. This chapter is dedicated to all of the people who do charity work, community work and volunteering work. They set amazing examples for us to follow, such as Mother Teresa, spiritual teacher - Zen Master Thich Nhat Hanh, Princess Diana, and of course my mum, Tu Nhien Ly. There are many more thousands of others that deserve recognition of course. I have listed only these names here as they have inspired and impacted me personally, and provided answers during my quest for happiness. This is my way of honouring their self-less work and amazing contribution to society and the world.

In this chapter I wish to discuss how fidelity relate to happiness.

According to the *Oxford Dictionary*, fidelity means *faithfulness to a person, cause, or belief, demonstrated by continuing loyalty and support.*

When I first think of fidelity, the thought begins with an individual, like our life partners. Like you and many others, I used to wonder at the age of 15, does love really last forever? Can we really have the 'happily ever after' life? And, does eternal love exist?

As I kept seeking for the meaning of life and searching for my happiness, I realised that, there isn't just me and him or you and I but there's all of us and I also realised the following:

While still young and in our school years, happiness is found in our friendships. If your best friend is upset, it upsets you.

While you are dating, if you get a 'broken heart', all your friends and family worry about you.

Once you are married, your happiness is not just about the two of you. There are the extended family related matters.

When we hear of unforeseen circumstances happening in our neighbourhood, in our community, or in other parts of the world, it also affects our inner peace and happiness.

Therefore fidelity is not just about two people. We are all linked to each other in one way or another. And, so, **I have discovered** that there is an *extended eternal love* that we have, apart from the parental eternal love, like the love that I still feel between my mum and me even though she is no longer physically here.

She has rested in peace for the past 13 years and yet I still feel connected to her and still feel her love and send her mine. I have been so inspired by my mum that I continue to look into what she did and the meaning of it all to this day, and that is the *extended eternal love we have as human beings* that I am talking about.

This extended eternal love is one that can be passed on for generations to come. As we have seen from Mother Teresa, for example. Her love for others will be passed on indefinitely.

"If we have no peace, it is because we have forgotten that we belong to each other."

— Mother Teresa

You see, each person that Mother Teresa helped and cared for, she planted the seed of love and compassion in them. That seed of love and compassion flourishes, lives on and gets passed on and on, generation after generation. This is what I call the *extended eternal love.*

I used to wonder, what drives an individual to do charity work? I would hear stories of Mother Teresa's work but it's not until you actually witness such self-less work in person that you see the magnitude of the meaning. When I saw my mum carried out her charity work so whole-heartedly, I would look back at Mother Teresa, then back again at my mum. I soon realised that the love these two mothers leave behind will go on indefinitely. Although probably no one has heard of my mum's name like Mother Teresa, her silent work has impacted others and she certainly had left a legacy of love and kindness, and devotion on this world for posterity, whether others know about it or not.

Happiness isn't all about the love between 'lovebirds'. If so, what happens when one of the two is gone? Does that mean that we can no longer find happiness ever again if we choose not to find another person to spend the rest of our lives with? There must be a greater love. Love that has no conditions. Love that has no limits, and love that lets us feel the true essence of joy and freedom. Love that is pure and warm.

While I couldn't ask the two amazing mothers who inspired me the most to share with you in their own words about this extended eternal love, as they are no longer here with us in physically form. I have asked the founding director and CEO of School for Life Foundation, Ms. Annabelle Chauncy OAM, to share with us her personal thoughts on contribution to others and happiness.

I have had the opportunity to meet Ms. Annabelle through my children's charity work. In 2016, my 8-year-old daughter and 11-year-old son did painting, sold raffle tickets, and collected donations both inside and outside of their school, and raised about $2,600 for the Starlight Children's Foundation. That was their third consecutive year of doing charity work to help raise funds for different causes. Annabelle certainly had inspired my children, Aaron and Jeslyn to see more meaning in contributing to others. She is a great example for them and has really confirmed and comforted them to see on a larger scale that their wish to contribute to others is a very valid cause. We were in awe with gratitude to hear of her journey in building the School for Life Foundation.

Below is the message I received personally from Ms. Annabelle:

"There's a saying that says 'give and you shall receive' but for me, everything I've given towards my charity School for Life Foundation, I've received back tenfold. There are no words to describe seeing a child who would otherwise never have had the opportunity to go to school, receiving a brand new uniform, their first ever piece of new clothing, and coming to school every day with an opportunity to learn. Education really is freedom for children in Uganda — the freedom to lift themselves out of poverty, disease and war. I've been lucky enough to witness the life-changing impact education has had on the lives of thousands and this service to humanity has driven my happiness. I'm not driven by material goods or words of appreciation; I'm driven by the smiles on the faces of children and adults receiving the lifelong, irrevocable gift of education. There are no words to describe this level of contentment."

Such acts of kindness illustrates to us that; it is not just our genes that make us who we are. It is not how we were conceived that makes us who we are. It is how we choose to live life that makes us who we are.

This is the kind of deep contentment and happiness that lasts - with such recognition for self-love and self-worthiness on the largest scale is what brings about ultimate happiness.

When we live life with purpose, which essentially is to serve others, for our family as well as the wider community, it makes us feel more complete because it helps us to feel that there is a circle of love that comes back to us in the end.

As you can see, once we have self-love, it is easier to continue extending that love to others and on to the universe at large. This does not mean we all have to drop everything to go and do charity work, as not everyone has the wherewithal to do so, yet, we all can contribute in our own way.

All we need to do is to bear compassion in our hearts, and contribute with the generosity from our hearts. It's about doing the smallest things we can to help another whenever we can. A simple smile can pass on the feelings of kindness. A helping hand when needed makes all the difference.

Your contribution can be in the smallest way and yet, the impact could be bigger than you would ever imagine. For example, taking a minute to direct someone who is lost, even though you're rushing, or offering to pick up groceries for an elderly neighbour, especially in extreme weather conditions. I am sure most of us do these little acts of kindness but we don't think much of it. A lot of people think of contribution as charity work or donating money. Well it doesn't always have to be, and it doesn't always have to involve raising funds. It's about having compassionate thoughts and extending kindness, and thinking of and for others.

Once you starting connecting sincerely, you will naturally embrace compassion and it will lead you to realise your life purpose, and your contentment. It is also very natural that you will think outside of yourself; to think of others, of the world, and to be continually contributing, such as, when you start thinking of the poor and hungry, of the less fortunate, you will suddenly realise that you have a lot more to give than you think you have. You will suddenly live from a place of abundance, rather than scarcity, because you will realise how much more you have than others.

For some individuals, once they realise that extended eternal love, they just can't resist the calling and suddenly, there seems to be this infinite power that is gifted to them to keep them striving and keep them going, as we can see from Mother Teresa's example.

You will gain the unstoppable energy required for this journey of serving your purpose for a better world. This is when you will feel true satisfaction on a larger scale, and you will experience the everlasting kind of happiness that brings about the deepest contentment as you share the extended eternal love with the world.

I heard the following statement in my early years from my parents: "We come to this world with empty hands and we will go with empty hands". Why then do we need to work so hard and to earn so much? Apart from having the luxury of comfort and wealthy status, at the end of the day, at the end of our life, it is all about self-worth, and the legacy you leave behind, of who you really are. Does that equal to self-identity? Not entirely. What happens when you lose all of your material wealth? What happens to identity then? Your identity should be who you truly are as a person. It's about the values you uphold and not what you have possessed or earned. This is the true reason why you need to connect authentically so that once disaster strikes, and if you were to leave this physical world immediately, you leave a legacy of who you really are and not what materials things you have possessed.

All the stress that comes with earning all the material possessions could be vanish in one hit of a natural disaster cause, if material possessions and achievement was what your happiness dependent on.

However, the achievements and contributions from our hard work signify and validate our dedication, the drive we have for our lives, and so my quest for happiness has led me to understand that the world would be a better place if we all simply lived by the thought that: "I will leave the world a better place than when I came". This way, we will feel more joy and peace. From that we will be able to pass on that joy we have received, creating a ripple effect that spreads joy and happiness, and eventually it comes back to us. Like a circle of love that has no end.

My greatest teachers and mentors have demonstrated this to me from an early age. My parents did many charitable works that no one actually saw or noticed at all. It was post-war time in Vietnam. My dad had a grocery store, and he would carry 50kg bales of rice to give to those in need. It was just a natural thing to do. You help whenever and wherever you can.

My mum was constantly helping others throughout her life in Vietnam, and after coming to Australia, she worked tirelessly with others at the temple to raise money in Sydney to send back to Vietnam to help the orphanage, and to provide medical help for those who have lost their eye-sight, or for those who needed eye operations but had no means to afford it. She worked tirelessly, even until her last day before she joined Buddha, during her trip back to Vietnam in 2004.

Both of my parents really demonstrated this *extended eternal love* for others and in doing so, provided great models for me to gain deeper understanding on happiness and contentment. I have come to the understanding that as we connect and share happiness with others, we will also bring about more inner peace and more inner joy to ourselves and others. Except, we must remember, *in order to pass on this extended eternal love, we need to connect with ourselves first to have self-love and self-worth.*

In reverse, if we were to serve in order to feel self-worth, then the energy will feel heavy because by then, we need other's love in order to feel self-love when they are the one who need it most, and we may not feel that level of deep contentment that we are seeking. *Therefore,* **we must find our self-love before we can contribute to others.**

It is our self-love, self-connection that is at the core of the happiness that we can turn to. It is our spirit, our soul. In the event that we have lost everything, we know that we are still okay. We still have that 'free', loving energy to share with others. It is unlimited and we have access to it immediately and infinitely. Self-love gives us access to happiness anytime, and all the time.

"Self-love and self-connection leads us to think of others, to work for others, and to serve others. Through this, we gain a deeper level of happiness and true contentment as we bring happiness to others. In the end, it reflects back to us with the love others have for us. This is when we complete the circle of love and how we can achieve true contentment and ultimate happiness."

— Linda Tomai Duong

"Ultimately, happiness begins from within us, then shared with others and all beings, and all the way to the universe, and ends with happiness coming back to us, completing the circle of love."

Linda Tomai Duong

Chapter 12

The Story Before the
Happiness Discovery

After moving to Sydney in 1985, I witnessed my mum devoting herself to visiting the Buddhist temple, and working very hard, participating in charity work. She was inspired to follow Buddha's footsteps, seeking enlightenment so that in the next life she wouldn't have to be reborn as a human being, and could stay in Nirvana, similar to how those who attend other churches, wish that their spirit will go to heaven after this life on earth. To the teenage me, at the age of 15, it had meant that she wanted *to be happy eternally.*

Religion aside, let me share with you a bit about my mum. She was a petite lady with her own charm. Her warmth radiated with energy that lit up any room she entered. Her gentle, cheerful and caring nature cheered up any sorrowful soul. She was often asked; "What cream do you use for your face? Your skin looks so shiny!"

Her answer was nothing except rice water to wash my face. Each time she prepared rice to be cooked, after she rinsed the rice, she would keep the water and use it to wash her face. That was what she thought had kept her facial skin so naturally beautiful and shiny. I used to believe that completely too. But now, I think it was also her warm and cheerful heart, her inner peace was what had contributed to her glowing face. It was also her beautiful, happy nature that contradicted her search for the ultimate happiness that made me become even more curious about life ahead of me.

She was one super nurturing mother, with 10 children under her wings, I still felt like the most special and only child, each time I was with her. Her complete presence would make me forget that I had nine other siblings to share her attention with.

At 70 years of age, she was still keen to attend English classes in Sydney. She often encouraged her friends to join her to attend classes, and their responses were; "We are too old to learn a new language," another said; "Why bother! We're so old already…!" Her replies were; "Oh well, we're only sitting at home doing nothing anyway. Why not just turn up? If we learn another word then we have another word to use." And it was with those replies that more and more friends had followed her, joining in the class. She was such a warm, quiet leader in her own quiet way. It was impossible not to be inspired by her. Then, come the moment she was awarded her graduation certificate for the English class. It was such a cute, sweet, and proud moment when you see your mum holding the certificate at the age of 70, smiling and proud!

How could she be unhappy when she had such drive throughout her entire life? I questioned this but only to realise later on that *she was in fact happy*, but *she had wanted her happiness to last even longer; to wanted it to last for forever! She had wanted to achieve true contentment — the actual, ultimate happiness; one that doesn't fade away. She had wanted her happiness to last eternally.*

Dealing with Cultural Differences

I too, started attending English as a Second Language (ESL) classes. This class was situated within a normal high school where we were able to spend time with the none-ELS students. One day, during recess, I was trying to wave at a classmate, wanting her to come and join me. I put my hand up, my palm facing towards her, and waved in an up and down motion, to signify a wave, calling her to me, just as we would wave someone over in Vietnam. Strangely, the minute she came over, she was grumpy at me and told me she was offended. "*Why did you wave at me like you're waving at a dog?*" I was so bewildered! I had no idea what she was talking about at the time; especially with my minimal spoken English. Not until later, when a Chinese-Vietnamese friend who had been in the ESL class much longer than me, told me that "If you want to wave for someone to come to you, you do it this way — you put your palm face up, and you curl the fingers towards yourself and you wave towards yourself. That's how you wave them to you." The hand gestures and their meanings in the two different cultures were completely opposite. From East to West many things are not just different but the exact opposite!

Apart from the huge cultural shock and the demands of adapting to the immense cultural differences, I also had to deal with my own growing, confusing years of being an awkward teenager.

Luckily, I had lots of love and support from my big, loving family, so I had lots of room in my heart and mind to grow and adapt. But for my mum, it was quite different. Her life was much more challenging; losing her mum at the mere age of eight years old, not much education opportunities, and raising 10 children in a resource limited country.

Having received so much love growing up, I just could not imagine what it would have been like as a child to grow up without a mother and yet, she still became such a compassionate, loving and cheerful person and mother despite all the of the hardships.

She was an amazing individual with amazing positive energy that radiated right from her heart each time she smiled. It never occurred to me to ask her this; how was she able to *choose* to be happy when life presented her with such tragedy by taking her mum away when she was so young? How did she *choose* to be happy when she had no mum to kiss her better after she had leeches all over her calves from working in the rice fields in those early years?

She had grown up in the countryside before moving to Ho Chi Minh City. Once we immigrated to Sydney, Australia, she took up learning English, so that she could live her life independently, for example, being able to direct a taxi driver to take her home from the shops, during those times when we were at school. She was amazingly adaptable and an extremely hard worker. Not to mention having to raise 10 children, which no doubt brought her many challenges and tribulations along the way. However, through all of these tests, mum showed herself to be an incredibly strong-minded individual with high emotional intelligence and resilience. She really was a super-mum in my humble opinion. I have total respect, love, and utter admiration for her, and that has reinforced my quest for true happiness. How could she have gone through so much in life and yet still displayed such a good and happy spirit? Yet, at the same time, she was still searching for a longer lasting kind of happiness. That was what intrigued me.

My mum encouraged and inspired me to search for the ultimate happiness. It was her amazing, determined, and bright spirit that gave me such phenomenal inspiration and led me on this journey to seek true contentment — *the essence to ultimate happiness* for myself and now sharing my journey with you. It was a quest that was instilled in me subconsciously without direct intention. It was almost like a "quiet" search that began in my mind early on.

Seek and You Will Find

After six months in the ESL class, we had to move on to a normal high school. Every day I went to school, I was super quiet as I had not yet learned enough English words to be conversational. I often looked down to my hands and fingers to avoid making eye contact, in case others wanted to start a conversation.

Each time I looked down, there were my hands. My palms were my only companion at the time. My mind would start to drift away and thoughts came in. All kinds of thoughts… "Where am I? Where are we? Why are we here, in a foreign country? Why do we always have to worry about money?" Back then, my sister and her then husband had taken on a huge financial responsibility in order to sponsor seven of us – mum and dad, and five of us to come to Australia from Vietnam. She had lived the life of a refugee, became a legal resident and Australian citizen, and worked incredibly hard in order to save up to afford seven air tickets. As well, they had a lot of living expenses while acting as financial guarantors for us all to come and live in Sydney. This responsibility burdened her with enormous amount of stress and pressure, while she was still adapting and building a new life for herself and her own new family. We are all forever grateful to her and her ex-husband for their brave, risk-taking spirit and all the sacrifices they have made.

However, I was too oblivious to consider such matters at that age; I was way too naïve and way too busy with my own wonderment. As I drifted away on my own thoughts and dreams, I often felt other's unhappiness and felt their need to feel happier. It made me wonder often and I would ask: "What is happiness and how can we have longer lasting feelings of happiness so that mum doesn't have to wait for Nirvana to experience it?" and "How can I make sister feel less stress and happier? (referring to the sister who had sponsored us here)." Every day, during school's break time, this self-dialogue seemed to go over and over in my head.

Eventually, after I was well settled in school and I had made some good friends, and started to get used to the new culture, I started to feel okay and became more relaxed. I was then able to 'park' these worrisome thoughts aside. I developed space in my mind for questioning and wonderment in a more relaxed state. I remember that day clearly; I was wearing the solid yellow shirt and ink blue pants of my school uniform, sitting on a bench at recess time; all on my own in a very quiet moment, looking down - I stared at my palms and started to name my fingers.

Picked on my thumb and named it — Family: Where love and safety come from.

Picked on my middle finger and named it — (Friends): For company and support.

Picked on my pointer and named it — Money (Finance): Can't be happy if we don't have the basics met.

Picked on my ring finger and named it — Fun (Fitness): I used to love bush walking, and going to the beach.

Picked on my pinkie and named it — Love life (Fidelity): Some people think it's a partner, some think it's their pets, some think of their children, and my mum was thinking of the universe; 10 children, the orphanage in Vietnam, the blind children and those with eye problems such as cataracts, the temple and Buddha.

I came to realise that these five elements were the basics that have contributed to my life's search for contentment and happiness. Although not exclusively confined to these five elements; I strongly believe that they provide a good foundation to one's happiness, and in achieving inner peace and inner joy - the ultimate happiness.

My thoughts were that I had a big loving family even though we were no longer in our birth country. "We are here. We belong to each other. I have great relationships with my siblings. I feel secure, protected, and all we need is to be *happy for longer periods of time*." Holding these five fingers together, it was just like a palm that holds the happiness together. That was the foundation for me to achieve happiness on a an on-going basis, and to make use of what I already had instead of searching for things that I could not gain access to since I was only 15 years old.

I didn't make many friends at first, as I was not very talkative at the time, mainly due to my limited English vocabulary and my shy, quiet nature. However, whenever I made friends, we would become good friends. The first friend that I made on the first day of my ESL class is still a close friend today, 32 years later. Throughout the first year of friendship, we used to call each other every day because we both spoke Cantonese to each other. I thank her often for our amazing friendship.

My other amazing 'first friend' that I have met on my first day at high school in Sydney, is my wonderful friend from Peru. This friendship has also lasted more than 30 years. Neither of us could speak English well at the time, but we connected really well and could communicate on a personal level that we both understood, respected and appreciated each other. We were the funniest looking pair of buddies in school! She was tall, slim and beautiful with red hair. I was petite with black hair. Amusingly, how we were able to be such good friends is still a mystery to the both of us. What is even more precious is that, more than a quarter of a century later, the friendship continues as if it was just yesterday.

Both of these friendships have contributed greatly to my ease of settling into this new country because of the genuine, authentic connection that we have made. The steady friendships gave each of us a sense of stability, which was most important in our growing years as we helped each other transitioned into the new country, embracing our new culture.

Gradually, I made more friends and many have developed into long lasting friendships spanning 10 to 20 plus years. Over the years, I have become more talkative and have lightened up. My friends often make me laugh as they have such a way of seeing lots of innocent humour in life. Sometimes I laugh so much that I get painful stitches in the back of my spine. Has that ever happened to you? You laugh so hard that your lower spine hurts? They can say the simplest things in the most innocent way and yet it is so funny! That is how much fun it is to be with my friends. Simple but joyful! Although we are older now, with more life concerns and worries, whenever we are together with our humorous mood kicked in, we're still guaranteed for our fun times and a 'laughter fix', for sure!

It is all about the connection and being genuine with each other, having trust, loyalty, and support for each other, while also respecting each other's differences. Both of these friendships have shown me a common element for developing forever friendships — the deep connection we have with each other.

Being deeply connected with my mum and happily and connecting with friends was when I truly started my journey on experiencing the joy and contentment needed for a happier life, regardless of our finances or circumstances. It was the deep connections that kept me happy.

Since that day in the school playground, when I first thought of the palm concept of the five 'Fs' that are listed above as the foundation elements for achieving happiness, it made me realised that we have happiness at our fingertips, and over the years, things have not changed my view, and during these discovery years, it has only re-emphasised to me more that these five foundational elements are what have contributed to my life's contentment as I connect to myself, with others and the universe, helping me to achieve inner calm, inner joy and ultimate happiness.

Happiness and contentment are already within us. If we just stay connected with our true self and have self-love to embrace the greater love — the love for others, love of nature and the love for the universe around us, we *will* achieve happiness and contentment in life. There is no need to seek outwardly but only inwards. Start connecting and you can access happiness right now, regardless of your financial status. Access the inner peace and inner joy in the small moments that life bring and happiness will follow. That is when you will feel *rich;* because happiness is the most treasured form of wealth.

Therefore…

The secret to living a happier life is Connection.

"Connection is the New Currency; The Secret to Ultimate Happiness."

Linda Tomai Duong

Chapter 13

The Five Fs

"Happiness is not a destination. Happiness is right here, right now. You can simply access happiness within you."

Linda Tomai Duong

Whenever you need a reminder as to where you are on the happiness journey, all you need is to look at your palm. You can access to your support systems; the five foundation elements of Family, Friends, Finance, Fitness and Fidelity.

We don't have to have all five elements all present at the same time:

If you don't have a Family: You can begin to make friends and become connected with them, whether at school, work or outside. Feeling love and having connections with others will help you feel better, more able to engage at school or at work, and will lead you to become more engaged in life, allowing you to feel more secure about the future ahead.

Simply by doing this, you will have already touched three elements; Family, Finance, Friends. Your school life falls under Finance, which represents achievement. Once you feel loved, connected and secure while achieving, then you are more inclined to start to think about others; doing good deeds, sharing and contributing, which in turn makes you feel even more complete.

If you don't have Finances: You can always turn to your family and friends for help and support, together with ideas and inspiration for creative thinking. This process can propel you to a place where you can start earning. Again, just keep connecting and be open for the helps that are coming your way. You never know where ideas and supports can lead you. In the meantime, do conscious breathing, eat well, drink lots of water, and get plenty of sleep and keep fit. Building healthy habits and keeping fit is not only about going to the gym. Get outdoors, bond with nature and stay positive. Connection with others and nature is where you begin.

If you don't have Friends: Start connecting with new people. Start with social media platforms if meeting people in person is difficult for you, slowly you can connect in person if possible. But remember to connect authentically and show who you really are for real friendships to be formed. The effort is worthwhile because when friends connect friends, and with the help of the internet, very soon, you will be connecting with the world.

If you don't have the physical Fitness levels that you want, it is okay: What's important is to do what you can and keep fit in your mind to be positive. Also, keep connecting with others, because happiness is not a destiny; you don't have to wait until you are fit or until you get 'there'. It is not governed by status, circumstances. Happiness is within us. We can access happiness any time we wish. All begins with connection.

If you want to feel Contributing: Start with compassionate thoughts from your heart. Remember that fidelity is about contributing to others in the smallest way you can, and it's about the extended eternal love that comes back to reflecting on the love we have for ourselves, for others, and from others.

It is not necessary to have all five elements in order to achieve true contentment and happiness. All we need to do is to keep connecting with others, natures and the universe. By realising and remembering what we already have, we can access our happiness. We no longer need to say "I'll be happy when…"

"Connection is the Secret to Ultimate Happiness."

— Linda Tomai Duong

"Connection
Is The Secret
To Ultimate Happiness."

Linda Tomai Duong

Chapter 14

Where Are You Now?

At this stage, I would like to sincerely say thank you for joining me on this journey of discovering deeper joy and inner peace from within.

Now I would like to invite you to pause, take a conscious breath, and take a moment to reflect on where you are now with your happiness journey. (1 is lowest, 10 is highest)

On a scale of 1-10 (1 is lowest, 10 is highest), mark where you were on the scale before reading this book? Please circle.

1   2   3   4   5   6   7   8   9   10

On a scale of 1-10 (1 is lowest, 10 is highest), mark where you are now after reading this book. Please circle.

1   2   3   4   5   6   7   8   9   10

Notes for yourself

What is your main take-away from this book?

_____

_____

_____

_____

_____

Is there someone you would like to make connections with immediately?

Write down their names:

_____

_____

_____

_____

_____

_____

What can you do differently to increase more connections at home, with friends, at work and in your community?

_____

_____

_____

_____

_____

_____

I would love to hear how this book has helped you to achieve more happiness. Please feel free to connect with me at: linda@lindaduong.com.au or linda@linkcoaching.com.au

Or visit my websites:

www.linkcoaching.com.au or www.lindaduong.com.au

To others I say:

"Happiness Is Another Form of Wealth!"

To myself I say:

"Happiness Is the most treasured Form of Wealth!"

Linda Tomai Duong

References

I would like to acknowledge the learning and wisdom from the elders and mentors of the past and present, and to all who have shared their life stories with me as an acquaintance, friend, or past clients, and current clients.

The sharing in this book is a recollection of my life learning thus far. Therefore it is impossible to list all the references as to whether it is a certain person, a certain book, movie or life events that I have learned a certain lesson from. I only read certain chapters of a book that resonated with me. Mostly the sharing of this book is based on my memories and recollection of my daily reflections.

Below are the few resources that I can list:

Below are the books that have inspired me most:

The Art of Power by Master Thich Nhat Hanh.

Chicken Soup for the Soul by Jack Canfield and Mark Victor Hansen

Who Moved my Cheese by Dr Spencer Johnson

Chapter 9

Emotional Intelligence definition

Harvard Business Review, written 28th April, 2015, retrieved on 28/08/17, from;

https://hbr.org/2015/04/how-emotional-intelligence-became-a-key-leadership-skill

Afterword

When I first embarked on searching for my happiness, I wished there was a book on the subject, telling me how I can achieve happiness in a simple way. As I looked and searched, back then, the books were written by the academia, the philosophers, and spiritual leaders, and they were way too heavy and way too complicated for my 15-year-old self with minimal English language skills, as I first immigrated to Sydney with not a word of English.

As the years went on, I first thought of writing this book only for my two children, to share with them the learning I had gained and to leave a legacy of their maternal grandma behind for them. However, as I embarked on the author journey, I signed up to different online writing courses, one of which was ran by Jack Canfield, the co-author of the *Chicken Soup for the Soul* series and Steve Harrison, the British copywriter, creative director. In one of the interviews shared as a resource for the students, Jack had said that his mentor had once advised him that: "If you cannot find the book that you're looking for, write it!" This message resonated with me right to my heart as that was what I was in the process of doing.

Soon, the need for me to share the messages of this book with the world became increasingly apparent. If I was needing it, then others must have needed it too. Life is complicated and there has more and more uncertainty happening around the world as the stories of terrorism and other disturbing news items flash across our screens. My concern is that all of these elements can disturb our inner peace and our inner joy.

Everything starts from us. One individual. One mind. World peace or terrorism; of course they are different acts, but both start from the mind, from inner-self. Just as this quote illustrates:

If there is to be peace in the world,

There must be peace in the nations.

If there is to be peace in the nations,

There must be peace in the cities.

If there is to be peace in the cities,

There must be peace between neighbours.

If there is to be peace between neighbours,

There must be peace in the home.

If there is to be peace in the home,

There must be peace in the heart.

— Lao Tzu

Every action stems from how we feel. Our thoughts and emotions are what drive us into taking actions.

Since the message of this book is all about reaching out to connect with others. In the resource section, you can connect with those professionals to help if you require their services to access happiness in a more practical way. Of course, you are more than welcome to access more help from me too through www.linkcoaching.com.au

Connection — The Currency to Happiness is certainly about my never ending quest of searching for happiness and world peace in a quiet yet most profound way. I will always be drawing on the Chinese philosopher - Lao Tzu's quote on this journey, so be sure to see more in depth editions as my author and life journey grow.

Acknowledgements

Thank you to my amazing parents; my dad, Binh Duong, and my mum, Tu Nhien Ly, No words could express my gratefulness for your nurturing love and support, and for all you do. I am forever in gratitude to be your daughter.

I would like to thank my second eldest sister, Lan and her ex-husband, Bill, for their bravery as they have risked their lives at sea to find a new world, found happiness for themselves and ultimately benefited the rest of their families as well, by sponsoring us to come as immigrants to Sydney, enabling us to have the opportunities we have enjoyed here, in this beautiful country called Australia.

I could not have experienced the joy and happiness in my growing years had I not had the love and care from my siblings. I have amazing support from each and every one of my nine brothers and sisters, in all different situations. Some are especially close due to the closeness of our age, yet the older ones are just as dear in my heart. I am grateful for all your love and support. I hope I have retold with as much accuracy as I can remember, of our family's selected old time stories, and about mum and dad, and that I have shared their teachings well.

Due to the 20-years age gap from my eldest sister, I had the honourable experience of being an aunt at the young age of five, which is almost unheard of. I embraced this status with pride, and carried out my duty appropriately as expected. I was proud and loved every moment spent connecting closely with all my nieces and nephews when they were babies, and at times even took on the parenting role in looking after them whenever the situation arose.

To all the people along the way, too many, some known, some unknown, whose insights and challenges, love and examples I have learned from and crossed paths with, each and every day that had enriched my life journey with, especially those whom have shared their personal stories with me such as Phoebe*. When I first came to think about writing the acknowledgements I became overwhelmed as to where to I begin with the list of people that had one way or another contributed to my life and happiness journey all these years.

I have made many long-term friends whom have all contributed to my happiness in one way or another, and it's impossible to list them all here. My two earliest friends after arriving in Australia; Vanessa C. and Silvina C., thank you for keeping our friendships alive and fresh as it was when we first met over 30 years ago. I always enjoy our laughter each time we meet up. To Bernice W. with whom I've shared the new motherhood journey since our boys were only four and six month old, thank you for all your prayers Bernice and Kevin.

I thank Mr. Rob W Stow for your enthusiasm and respect for my work. Not many authors have the courage to share their very first, raw, and unedited draft. Especially on such a topic, and I am glad I did - when it was at only 15,000 words. I really appreciated you took time to read it. I would also like to thank Mr. Andrew Gomes, my Toastmasters club mentor's support, who is always positive and encouraging.

I thank the teachers and mentors who have inspired me greatly; we have shared much joy and happiness together. Mrs. L. Andrews, my very first English teacher in the ESL class, who inspired me and showed me what a great, loving, selfless teacher is like. Mr. D. and Mrs. D. Daveport for loving me like their own daughter, and Mr. J. Carden, who has always seen the potential in me in whatever I do throughout the different careers I have transitioned into. Mrs. J. Collins, who is my children's teacher and has let us share much joy with her in our time together. It is so precious that I am able to share much happiness with each and every one of these great teachers and mentors. (I have not mentioned full names here to protect their privacy).

My thanks also go to all who helped with publishing this book. Viki Winterton from Expert Insights for her expert guidance and for being so patient with me throughout the publishing process of this book. I really appreciate all your help and support. Lynda

Dyer for the connections. My editors at different stages of my author journey. My latest editor, Amanda Webb, for your enthusiasm for me and my work. Your professional passion for this project and speedy response was exactly what I needed at the time. I have added more writing after your editing job was done, and so I assume the responsibilities for all errors there may be in this book.

I thank the guest experts who are featured in the resource section of this book for seeing my vision and for trusting in me, to provide the opportunity for greater connections to occur.

Thanks to my husband, Jason Lim for helping with the creative design of the book cover, and Julia Kuris for the technical design of the cover.

Thank you to Ms. Annabelle Chauncy OAM, the Founding Director & CEO of School for life for your precious time in sharing your very personal thoughts and messages on contribution to others and happiness.

Last but not least, my very personal thanks to my amazingly supportive husband, Jason, who supports me in everything I do, as I transition from one career to another, and thank you so much for your love and dedication to our little family. To my amazingly outstanding and loving children, Aron and Jeslyn, whom behave so incredibly maturely for their age, Thank you for your love, kisses, and hugs every day, and for your understanding and support always even at such young age. I love you both so dearly and so deeply.

To my readers for connecting by purchasing and reading this book. *Namaste!*

Thank you for following me on this journey, and for allowing me to share with you my little passages in my life. "We're all travelling through time together, in every day of our lives. All we can do is do our best to relish this remarkable life!"

With best wishes to all for your happiness,

— Linda Tomai Duong

Resources for More Connections

Following are the guest experts I have interviewed as the services that they provide are directly relating happiness.

Julie Ann

Business name; Julieann.co

Business Email address; Julie@julieann.co

Business phone number; +65 9843 0317

Linda; Please share with us a short summary of you and your services, as I understand your work ultimately contributes to happiness and peace in the mind.

Julie Ann; Thanks Linda – I'm a Spiritual/Meditation teacher, Intuitive Healer and Author ... currently based in Singapore. I offer a range of workshops and sessions (on-line and in person) to help people come back to centre and reconnect with their inner source of guidance, power and happiness.

Linda; How did you come to your passion and purpose in life?

Julie Ann; I suffered through a High Anxiety condition that peaked after a series of challenges that pushed it to the surface. Finally I couldn't ignore it! - So I embarked on a healing journey that included meditation and holistic therapies. Many years later I am now blessed to be a healer/teacher helping others on their own journeys back to balance and happiness. At a time where so many are dealing with anxiety, I'm so grateful to be able to offer hope, guidance and a pathway back to joy.

Linda; What help you achieve and maintain your happiness?

Julie Ann; A "non-negotiable" daily practice of meditation … and gratitude. Gratitude/Appreciation, for me, is the secret key to happiness.

Linda; what are your favourite tips?

Julie Ann;

1. Do something first thing in the morning to set your energy for the day. Happiness attracts more happiness (peace more peace) etc. so it's the best time to meditate or focus on positive intentions.

2. Do your practice daily to keep the positive momentum going and strengthen your connection to spirit/soul.

3. Amp up your daily gratitude journaling by adding a BECAUSE component to your gratitude declarations.

Eg. "I'm so grateful to Linda for including me in this book BECAUSE I get to collaborate with likeminded co-creators while sharing this powerful information with so many more people."

Make sure you read back your statements and feel the emotion/energy of the gratitude and the BECAUSE. You'll be amazed at how good this makes you feel and the energy itself helps to magnetise more good into your life. Write 10 of these statements a day and watch your life change before your eyes.

Linda; what impact would you like to see your work has on the world?

Julie Ann; An empowered society of co-creators where each person truly understands that the key to happiness is in their own hands.

Linda; How can our readers connect with you?

Julie Ann; Via my website www.julieann.co
OR my Facebook pages (I'm there interacting every day at www.facebook.com/lookingforasign)

Linda; Thank you for your time and for being featured here in this book.

Thank you for inviting me – Grateful ☺

Dr. Judith Boice, N.D., L.Ac., FABNO

Business name; Seven Winds Institute, Inc.

Business address; 846 SW Beaver Lane, Madras, OR 97741, USA

Business email address; drjudith@drjudithboice

Business phone number; +1 (541) 475-2131

Linda; Please share with us a short summary of you and your services, as I understand your work ultimately contributes to happiness and peace in the mind.

Dr. Boice; I am a naturopathic physician, acupuncturist, Fellow of the American Board of Naturopathic Oncology, award-winning author, and international teacher. My mission is to help people know what being healthy is for them, so they can focus on what is most important, whether that is riding bikes with their grandchildren, running three Iron Man competitions a year, or overcoming cancer. I consult with private patients, writes books, and offers trainings that teach people with chronic illness how to increase their energy, reduce symptoms and reverse disease by restoring their health with natural medicines. I believe the health of Earth, body and spirit are completely interdependent.

Linda; How did you come to your passion and purpose in life?

Dr. Boice; On a wilderness backpacking trip when I was 16 years old, I experienced how EVERYTHING around me was alive, including myself. That profound understanding in the Wind River Mountains of Wyoming (in US) changed my life. When I returned home, I was unable to sleep indoors for several weeks. That experience of the oneness of all life began to seep into every moment and every decision I made, including what I studied and the profession I chose.

Linda; What help you achieve and maintain your happiness?

Dr. Boice; Spending time in silence and in wilderness are very important to me. I also love music and have a background as a classical violinist. I find myself smiling when I begin to play my violin! I am about 49% artist/musician/writer and 51% doctor/healer, and I require giving attention to both of those major aspects of my soul on a regular basis.

Linda; what are your favourite tips?

Dr. Boice; Spend time outside every day, in wild places if possible. If you live in a city, walk or sit in a park, or even visit with a single tree. I also have a birdfeeder where I can watch the birds when I am unable to go outside.

Sun Bear, a Chippewa elder and teacher, taught me to put a bit or cornmeal in my pocket and wander until I found a place that felt "right," that called me to sit down. I would offer cornmeal and prayers for that place, for people I love, for wisdom I might be seeking; then, I would sit in silence, listening and being with that place. Often wisdom comes in the form of sudden insights, quiet feelings, words, or inspirations. Sometimes the answer comes later, in a seemingly random moment, after I have planted the "seed" of a request and made myself ready to hear a response.

For women, slow down and take quiet time for yourself during your menstrual bleeding, especially the first day. In some traditional cultures women went to the moon lodge to join other women during their bleeding time. In these cultures, women understood that they were much more sensitive during their bleeding time. The veils between the worlds are thinner, and therefore wisdom is much closer and easier to discern. Many Hopi prophecies, for example, came to women during their moon time (i.e. menstrual bleeding), along with new skills, new insights, and new ways of doing things. Each menstrual cycle is an opportunity to deepen your wisdom and "mature" on your journey to becoming an honoured elder.

Linda; what impact would you like to see your work have on the world?

Dr. Boice; In my work I aim to seed the understanding that our bodies are our Earth. Our bodies are the part of the planet we are most directly responsible for. I also offer the awareness of Green Medicine, a system of healing that supports the life, health, and diversity of our bodies AND the Earth's body. Green Medicines are of the Earth, by the Earth, and for the Earth, and they improve both personal and planetary health. I educate people about death and dying so they understand the dying process and can die consciously, comfortably and peacefully, with minimal or no pain medication. This peaceful passage helps position them for the most auspicious entry into whatever comes next on their soul's journey. Finally, I provide a new medical paradigm that shifts away from addressing symptoms to *creating health.*

Linda; How can our readers connect with you?

Dr. Boice; Please visit my website, www.drjudithboice.com

To apply for a free 45-minute consult on your next steps in creating your vision of health, visit:
https://app.acuityscheduling.com/schedule.php?owner=133782 22&calendarID=1254736

Linda; Thank you for your time and for being featured here in this book.

Dr. Boice; Linda, thank you for your passion and expertise in creating this book, and your patience with me in responding to this questionnaire!

Melody Chadamoyo

Business name; Heart Passion Institute

Business address; 5 Oakdale Grove, Ballycullen, Dublin 24

Business Email address; melody@heartpassioninstitute.com

Business phone number; +353 87 959 6258

Linda; Please share with us a short summary of you and your services, as I understand your work ultimately contributes to happiness and peace in the mind.

Melody; I help women know exactly who they need to be and what they need to do to have a joyful long lasting relationship.

Linda; How did you come to your passion and purpose in life?

Melody; I nearly got a divorce because I was so unhappy but instead I went on a journey to discover what makes relationships work well. The journey has caused a transformation that allowed me to accept my feminine elegance and understand men a lot better. The more I asked for what I needed the more my husband was more loving and caring towards me.

Linda; What help you achieve and maintain your happiness?

Melody; Being authentic and looking after myself both spiritually and physically helps me to feel happy all the time. I am a homing bird for joy which means I only do those things that give me more joy and happiness.

Linda; what are your favourite tips?

Melody; Allow yourself to be more feminine especially when you're dealing with a masculine man. Connect to your heart and approach yourself and everyone with a loving heart. Give yourself those things you wish other people would give to you. Men and women are not the same at all because they see the world very differently. Understanding that will help you to create a happier partnership. Sex is a spiritual connection so approaching it from a place of gifting benefits you a great deal. Nothing is worth doing if you're not enjoying it. There is no prize for suffering.

Linda; what impact would you like to see your work has on the world?

Melody; I want people to stop approaching relationships from a place of lack and fear and to rise up their love consciousness so they enjoy a more fulfilling unconditional way of loving.

Linda; How can our readers connect with you?

Please visit my website; https:heartpassioninstitute.com

Or Facebook page;
https://www.facebook.com/melodyp0/?ref=aymt_homepage_pa nel

Linda; Thank you for your time and for being featured here in this book.

Aurelie Catherine Cormier

Business name; Beyond Cancer Survival: Parenting for Health

Business address; Needham, MA USA 02492

Business Email address; AurelieCormier1@gmail.com

Business phone number; +1 617-417-8482

Linda; Please share with us a short summary of you and your services, as I understand your work ultimately contributes to happiness and peace in the mind.

Aurelie; Life is full of challenges. There are some things in life which are out of our control but there is much in life that is within our control. When we are aware of the simple strategies that can promote lifelong good health, then we can have a better chance of a healthful life that allows us to meet life's challenges with less pain, struggle and challenges, and more opportunities for adventure, fun and happiness. I want to bring to parents all the tools available to them through educational resources to give their children and themselves the best chance of a healthful and happy life by offering them the control to maintain good health.

Linda; How did you come to your passion and purpose in life?

Aurelie; I have always had a passion for prevention since I was a young child; it became imprinted into every cell of my body. In 1958, my uncle, who was 19 at the time, needed open heart surgery at Children's Hospital in Boston. He underwent successful surgery followed by a yearlong recovery. As he was regaining his strength, I was learning to walk and talk. We would take him out for a walk every day over that year. My whole family started a Healthy Heart Lifestyle that I live to this day. As a teen, I was aware that my purpose was to help others learn to help themselves. As an adult, that has evolved into teaching others how to help themselves maintain health and to prevent or reduce disease.

Linda; What helped you to achieve and maintain your happiness?

Aurelie; True happiness is a process. Earlier in my life I was more focused on my challenges. In my mid-twenties, I realized that I was creating many of my own challenges and life didn't need to be so painful. I began to understand that I had a choice. I began to look for role models of those who seemed to have a knack for a peaceful, fun and abundant life. When I was pregnant, I connected with a dear friend whose first baby died at birth. It became her life's mission to help other women have a positive experience in childbirth. I took lessons from her in Self-Attunement Meditation and it has been a transformative process for me. It has led me to be more heart-centered, more authentic, and happy. I am truly grateful to this woman and feel blessed that she crossed my path and we connected at just the right moment that made a difference for my life. I hope to pass it forward to others.

Linda; what are your favourite tips?

My tips can be summed up by following the acronym W.E.L.L.N.E.S.S. W.orking E.very L.iving day towards L.ove N.utrition E.xercise S.erenity and S.pirituality. Follow that and your whole family will have a greater chance of life long health!!

Linda; what impact would you like to see your work has on the world?

Aurelie; "My dream is to build a worldwide community of like-minded parents who have a Focus on Prevention and want to give their kids and grandkids a better chance at a healthier, happier life."

Linda; How can our readers connect with you?

Aurelie; You can connect with me through my website www.beyondcancersurvival.com and my Facebook page: https://www.facebook.com/BeyondCancerSurvival/

Linda; Thank you for your time and for being featured here in this book.

Rosa Garcia ND, CNC, CECP, EOC

Business name: Vital Care

Business email address: rgarciand@gmail.com

Business phone number: +1 718 991 1793

Business address: 1115 Broadway 11th floor New York, NY 10010

Linda; Please share with us a short summary of you and your services, as I understand your work ultimately contributes to happiness and peace in the mind.

Rosa: For many years, I have had the privilege of assisting many bodies heal themselves. It is wonderful and awe-inspiring to say the least. I stress to my clients how wonderfully our bodies are created — respect it. The services offered in my office include: Iridology, which helps me to see weaknesses in the body; Emotional Balancing, which is where trapped emotions can prevent us from healing and moving on with our lives, I help them identify the emotions and release them; Zyto is a bio feedback that picks the correct nutrition, herbs, essential oils, homeopathic and more for a person's specific body; Sclerology, the examination of the white of the eye as well as detoxing and nutrition. I also give seminars to educate on how our bodies function, nutrition, essential oils, et cetera and have recently added a new certification to my portfolio, as a Certified Essential Oils Coach.

Linda: How did you come to your passion and purpose in life?

Rosa: I was exposed to herbs as a child. My mother and great grandmother cured me of asthma. I can still proudly say to this day I have not had another attack. However, my journey began in my thirties when I became bedridden for one year due to an illness that no doctors were able to identify. I met an iridologist, who later became my mentor, and she immediately knew the reason for my illness. In two months I was out of bed and, upon her urging, I began to focus on holistic medicine to help others not to go through what I have.

Linda: What helps you to achieve and maintain your happiness?

Rosa: The joy of seeing people finally getting an answer to the 'why'. That to me is priceless. I suffered for a year and I know the frustration. I'm always happy when I see my clients improve, whether it's emotionally and/or physically.

Linda: What are your favourite tips?

Rosa: Find out your 'Why'. Why do you want to do what you do? When your answer is to bring joy to someone and you love what you do — do it. You can't go wrong. In the beginning people won't know you but when they see and feel your passion they will come.

Linda: What impact would you like to see your work have on the world?

Rosa: For everyone to understand that our bodies are amazingly created. They have control over what they place in and on their bodies. They *can* change how they feel and think. It is not beyond their reach.

Linda: How can our readers connect with you?

They can reach me at Vital Care on the contact details above or visit the website at: www.vitalcare-rg.com

Linda; Thank you for your time and for being featured here in this book.

Nuno Leitao

Business name; Nuno Leitao

Business address; Maidstone Road, Norwich, NR1 1EA, United Kingdom

Business Email address; anunoleitao@gmail.com

Business phone number; +44 75 3207 2650

Linda; Please share with us a short summary of you and your services, as I understand your work ultimately contributes to happiness and peace in the mind.

Nuno; I work with problem gamblers. They have been living a "fake" happiness as gamblers. I try to empower them to leave gambling behind and find true happiness.

Linda; How did you come to your passion and purpose in life?

Nuno; I had been working in the care sector for 6 years, which I loved immensely. Then I thought there must be more I can do to help people. So I met with a career's adviser and counselling came up as a suggestion for a careers path....I hadn't even considered this option, but it appealed greatly and I immediately embraced it full heartedly.

Linda; what helps you achieve and maintain your happiness?

Nuno; A positive attitude, paired with an understanding that the problems of the past can't be a life sentence but more a learning curve which leads to happiness and contentment. This is enhanced by the loving relationship I have with my family and partner.

Linda; what are your favourite tips?

Nuno; If you're feeling down let yourself go down as far as possible, then think of a moment in your past life that was good, extremely good, then weigh up the two feelings but chose the good one; use that as the energy to take you back up, out of the downward spiral.

Linda; what impact would you like to see your work has on the world?

Nuno; I would like a world where gambling is under control. Unlike other addictions, where your body will stop you from going any further, gambling has no physical side effects. So there needs to be limitations in place, where paying just for entertainment would keep everyone in a safe gambling environment and within their means.

Linda; How can our readers connect with you?

Nuno; They can visit my blog, www.nunoblog.com

Linda; Thank you for your time and for being featured here in this book.

Albert Salmani

Business name; envisionyournext.com - Life coach, Master NLP Practitioner and trainer

Business address; 3498 cherry ave San Jose Ca, 95118 United States.

Email address; albert@envisionyournext.com

Business phone number; (408)623-0280

Linda; Please share with us a short summary of you and your services that is directly relating to happiness.

Albert; I am ethnically Assyrian/Armenian, I was born and raised in Iran. In 1991 I migrated to U.S. currently living in California with my wife and two kids. I teach people how to get rid of their limiting beliefs and create a compelling vision and progress towards it, because progress equals happiness.

Linda; How did you come to your passion and purpose in life?

Albert; Marital and relationship challenges made me very desperate to seek answers, I was stuck and very unhappy with my life. But I knew there is an answer out there so I started searching and I end up finding my purpose in life.

Linda; What help you achieve and maintain your happiness?

Albert; Hunger has been the starter for any kind of achievement in my life and progress is what makes me go further and further.

Linda; what are your favourite tips?

Albert; "Every day is a new life for a wise man." Horace

"All life asking us is, to make a measurable progress in a reasonable time." Jim Rohn

"There is no way to happiness, happiness is the way." Wayne Dyer

"Either you run your life or others will run it for you." unknown

Linda; what impact would you like to see your work has on the world?

Albert; I really want to influence people to have a change of heart, we all know so much yet we feel very little.

Linda; How can our readers connect with you?

Send me an E-mail through www.envisionyournext.com, calling me directly or any other social media like FB etc.

Linda; Thank you for your time and for being featured here in this book.

About the Author

"Quietness is one of the most precious element

In nurturing the mind to activate its power."

— Linda Tomai Duong

Linda Tomai Duong

Linda Duong is a motivational speaker, author, life coach and thought leader in happiness and connection. She is an in-demand life coach who has helped many of her clients to attain and re-ignite their happiness by connecting with themselves, with others and with the universe.

Linda has been interviewed by industry peer leaders in the field of life coaching and featured on national television, global radio broadcasts, and in leading newspapers and magazines. She has travelled the world and connects with multicultural individuals and groups beyond the spoken language.

Linda's mission in life is to be known for inspiring others to become more than what they thought they could be, and to help them attain their ultimate happiness, because to others Linda says "Happiness Is Another Form of Wealth." To herself Linda says; "Happiness Is the Most Treasured Form of Wealth."

Linda's Motto

"Always Follow Your Dreams, Bring Joy to Others and Be Happy!"

Linda Tomai Duong

"We only live once. Make it count. Live a life with no regrets," are the words that have rung in my ears since I was 15 years old.

Born during the end of the Vietnam War, soil and sticks were the children's toys. I don't really remember having any plastic toys. Daydreaming was something I did frequently, at any opportunity. At the age of five, I dreamed of making beautiful dresses. At the age of seven, I dreamed of seeing the world. "What is America like?" and "What is Australia like?" were questions that had me daydreaming, every day. At the age of 10, I was inspired to become a teacher and to help others learn too. At the age of 15, after immigrating to Sydney, Australia, with not a word of English, I wondered how artists took part in art exhibitions because I don't remember ever having coloured pencils as a child.

Those dreams have led me to study in each field and achieve all my three early childhood dreams; I travelled the world, became a successful wedding gown designer, happy as a teacher, and more. No words can describe how grateful I am, to be able to live a life filled with love and passion. And with each career transition I made, I not only brought friends along with me on my journey, I also served others with my passion and purpose as I experienced the journey myself. To this day, as I follow all of my dreams, I strive to bring more joy to others, and to be happy within myself so that others can be inspired to live a happy life too.

The joy shared being a travel consultant

When I worked as a travel consultant, I brought friends along the journey with me. They too joined the industry and also benefited greatly from the opportunity to travel the world. At first I shared my joy of travelling and seeing the world with one client at a time. Each person that I saw and booked flights, accommodation, car hire and so on for, I brought joy to them and their family. Soon, I was appointed to do group bookings, and then was in charge of Asia Pacific tour bookings within a European tour company. I loved helping others to travel and see the world as I accomplished my dream of seeing the world myself.

The joy shared from owning my bridal boutique

I opened a bridal boutique in 2001, it was also the year that I married my husband. I understood exactly how a bride felt. I helped each bride to coordinate her dress for her perfect wedding setting, be it a church or a beach location. I was also able to make sure the entire bridal party, including the groomsmen and the mothers of the brides, looked great and were happy for the occasion. I took great care in helping my clients to mitigate any stress in the process of selecting the right gown for each individual. Making sure the mother of the bride felt respected and that the matron of honour received the right amount of attention yet did not overshadow the bride's day, that was all in a day's work, as well as helping the bridal party to stay calm, and reduce any anxiety and conflicts that may arise over the agreement of colour and style selections for the bridesmaids. I was supposed to be selling the dresses only, but in reality I was consulting and coordinating the whole bridal party.

There are many fond memories, two that stay with me most prominently. A beautiful and tall woman with a strong, healthy and very well-proportioned physique came in and said: "My baby is due in two weeks, but I don't want to look pregnant on my wedding day. Also, I want to have sleeves to cover my upper arms so that I look slimmer. I want to have Swarovski crystals and lots of pearls on my chest area. I looked all over Sydney but all the dresses I liked were way over my budget." At the time, my boutique was quite new but referrals were coming in already and normally, clients had to book six months in advance. I pushed everything aside. I designed and created the dress she so lovingly described, and completed and delivered her gown with an extra gift — a matching shawl to keep her warm as it was an autumn wedding. This was all delivered within her budget. The bride's sheer joy and the joy that I received was what I worked so hard for. As she wished, that day, the bride did not look so pregnant and yet magically that night on her wedding day, her baby girl was born. Just as well they had a day time wedding ceremony. That was in 2002.

My second fondest memory was a bride from the wonderful affluent suburb of Neutral Bay in Sydney. She wanted to walk down the church aisle with a grand, formal look and yet needed the practicality of a light and easily managed gown to board a helicopter flight immediately after the church ceremony. The consultation ended up with a modern, soft and slinky, backless gown with a sweeping train that was accentuated by a five-metre long veil and a pair of shiny satin gloves. This ensemble was offset by a glamorous, carefully selected tiara encrusted with Swarovski crystals and an outstanding choker that would rival any royal bride. On her last fitting, she was so overjoyed that she had to lie down for a few minutes before she could stand up and continue to admire herself in the mirror. I was able to serve the unity of families as she was able to meet her family's expectation of walking down the church aisle, as well as her own wish of boarding the helicopter flight with ease and grace.

During this career, I had also had the pleasure of inspiring others to start their own businesses and supported them when they needed it.

The joy shared from the parenting journey

When had my first child, I understood how challenging it was for other new mums, so I shared my journey and supported other mums to reach out and share the journey of new motherhood together. By the time I had my second child, I was inspired by my own children's deep curiosity for learning, which led me to look into Gifted Education and back to my childhood dream of studying teaching and becoming a teacher.

However, as my daughter began the kindergarten year at school, I volunteered three times a week to help out in the classroom, and I soon realised that children need great support from their parents. Soon after that, I also worked casually at a local pre-school and the same message surfaced, that teachers can teach as much as they love to at school, yet, ultimately children still need help and support at home, from their parents and carers. Through my own parenting journey, and as my children's first teacher, I was able to inspire and support other mums to enjoy their own motherhood journey more. I had always loved connecting and helping others. It was therefore only a matter of time before I would embark on the journey of working as a life coach professionally.

The joy I shared as a life coach

Working as a life coach focusing on the areas of parenting coaching and solo-preneur coaching was a natural progression for me as I desired to help others achieve their dreams too. In 2016, I flew to America to train as a life coach.

Below are a few testimonials to share with you, to illustrate how by using my intuition and enquiring nature I was able to help others identify the innate talents, dreams and potential they each had buried within and were able to explore with my help:

"Linda, you certainly have a gift for intuiting who needs your help, when they need it, and how to ask the right questions to help a person uncover (or at least get closer to) their own truth. Not only is your intuition and timing impeccable, but you also asked such genuinely caring, open-ended questions, which encouraged me to look deeper within for the clarity and confidence I needed in articulating my vision. Your simple yet highly effective way of coaching through casual conversation is something from which anyone can benefit. You were consistent in asking direct, open-ended questions, which gradually quelled most of my fears."

— Ashley S.

"Linda is masterful at listening at an intimate level. Personalised, uplifting and life giving perspectives are her gift to the world. She can lead you back to yourself in a very loving and tangible way, and easily sees and supports the vision you hold for yourself."

— Cherith K.

"My session with Linda was for the purpose of getting more clarity for my tutoring business. She was able to ask me specific questions that enabled me to clarify the business's main goals and vision. This was useful to determine the end goal of the business. It was an enjoyable conversation that enabled me to gain deeper clarity for my business."

— Jeryee L.

"I went through life thinking that I knew everything. I also thought that I have been a good mum to my three kids. I have spent my whole adult life looking after them and have always put them first before myself. I was oblivious to how they felt and what their views were towards me. After a few sessions with Linda, I learnt to let my kids grow and think on their own. I was able to give them the space they needed to be independent learners and to encourage them to find their own strengths and talents."

— Jacki N.

Standing by my mission

"Always Follow Your Dreams, Bring Joy to Others and Be Happy!"

Realising that there are no limits to achieving dreams, and that no matter what I do as a profession, whether I do motivational speaking these days or write books, it is just a different "vehicle" I use. My purpose and mission in life is to bring joy to others, whether that be through sharing joy at a one-on-one level or in a group setting or through my books. As my career paths evolved, my purpose has been the same, and that is to inspire and bring joy and happiness to others through my work. Hence, one of my own favourite quotes is: "Happiness Is the most treasured Form of Wealth!"

Throughout these pages, my hope has been to share the stories of my journey, my insights in experiencing happiness; the inner joy and inner peace even when life presents adversities, from the learning and wisdom in the Eastern culture, in my early childhood days in Vietnam and the Western teaching that I have learned while growing up and living in Australia nowadays - to help you open your heart and mind, to re-ignite and access your happiness right here, right now, as you read, and reconnect with yourself, and connect with the stories in this book. You are welcome too, to connect with me and share your happiness journey with me.

"Together, we connect and bring more happiness to the world!"

www.ingramcontent.com/pod-product-compliance
Lightning Source LLC
Chambersburg PA
CBHW062152270326
41930CB00009B/1509